MANAGEMENT:

Tidbits for the New Millennium!

by
Maxwell Pinto

Strategic Book Publishing
New York, NewYork

Copyright © 2009

All rights reserved – Maxwell Pinto
No part of this book may be reproduced or transmitted in any form or by any means, graphic, electronic, or mechanical, including photocopying, recording, taping, or by any information storage retrieval system, without the permission, in writing, from the publisher.

Strategic Book Publishing
An imprint of Writers Literary & Publishing Services, Inc.
845 Third Avenue, 6th Floor – 6016
New York, NY 10022
http://www.strategicbookpublishing.com

ISBN: 978-1-60860-084-7
SKU: 1-60860-084-X

Printed in the United States of America

Book Design: Bonita S. Watson

Dedication

TO MY FAMILY and friends who have always encouraged me to write books on the subject of management. Hopefully, this book will benefit students, lay people, and professionals alike.

During the preparation of this book, several books were reviewed and lost due to an unfortunate incident. I thank the publishers and authors of those books and sources that I accessed on the Internet and I apologize for not being able to include their names in this bibliography.

Preface

THIS IS MY third book on management. This book is meant to provide easy reading for those interested in grasping the essentials of general management, business ethics, Japanese management, trade unions, women in the workplace, and business continuity planning—in a nutshell.

The first and second editions of this book were reviewed by businessmen, professionals, students, and others. What follows is a revised edition based on feedback and review by the individuals in question.

In the new millennium, life in business and elsewhere is expected to be volatile and increasingly complex. The essentials of management were covered in my previous books, namely, *The Management Syndrome: How to Deal with It!* and *Management: Flirting with Disaster!* both of which represent detailed approaches to management and are available through Amazon.com and RoseDog Books Online.

This book aims to highlight other areas—business ethics, Japanese management, trade unions, women in the workforce, and business continuity planning—and to provide management tidbits relating to certain issues faced in the corporate world.

Acknowledgments

MANY THANKS TO Maurice Pinto; Mark Pinto, MBA, ChFC; Jim Stanton, training consultant; Krishna Prasad, BSc; Aley Thomas, MBA; Eusebia Menezes-Pinto, MA, MSc; Damian Lobo, BA; Josie Gelacio, BEd; Mari-jane Sutton; Aaron Pinto; Komal Jackson; Ranu Maharaj, Ben Percic; and others whose names I may have overlooked but to whom I am eternally grateful.

Contents

Dedication .... *iii*

Preface .... *v*

Acknowledgments .... *vii*

Chapter 1 1
Some Tidbits,
Introduction, Effective Leadership: A Torch Which Must Be Passed On!, Interviewing, Listening, Mentoring, Motivation, Conflict Management, Consultants, Customers, Delegation, Rights of Appeal, Diversity in Organizations, Intercultural Communication, Employee Assistance Programs, Special Needs/Mentally or Physically Challenged Individuals, AIDS, Substance Abuse, Organizational Policies, Ethics, Family-Friendly Management, Feedback, Innovation and Creativity, Negotiation, Networking, Organizational Culture, Orientation of New Employees, Politics in Organizations, Public Relations, Sexual Harassment, Stress Management, Teamwork, Total Quality Management, Termination of Employees and Restrictions, Training, Employee Turnover, Violence in the Workplace, Virtual Management, Conclusion and Summary

Chapter 2 23
Japanese Management: For Better, for Worse
The Japanese Economic Miracle, Lifetime Employment, The Godfather System, Is Japan One Big Firm?,

Lessons to be Learned from the Japanese, Some Perplexities in Japan, Industrial Relations in Japan, Quality: An Overall Emphasis, Conclusion

Chapter 3 35
Trade Unions: A Necessary Evil?
Objectives of the Business Enterprise, Developing a Relationship with Freelancers, A Labor Union, Conciliation and Mediation, When All Else Fails, Some Issues in Collective Bargaining, Open Book Management (OBM):Sharing Information with Employees, Conclusion and Summary

Chapter 4 41
Women: From Here to Eternity!
Women: The Good, the Bad, and the Ugly, Men: The Good, the Bad, and the Ugly, Women of the Old-School Genre, Women of the New-School Genre, Positive Effects of the Evolution, Negative Effects of the Evolution, Politics Then, Politics Now, Power in the Hands of Women: To Use or to Abuse?, Professional Women: Independent and Single versus Independent and Married, The Ladder of Success: Barefoot and Pregnant to Chairperson of the Board, The Educated Woman, Other Matters for Consideration, Conclusion

Chapter 5 51
Business Continuity Planning: A Team Approach, Introduction and Objective, Approach, Management Commitment: An Absolute Must!, Critical Business Functions, Risk Assessment and Business Impact Analysis, Disaster Tolerance: Closing the

Freshness Window, The Delphi Method, Controls, Documentation and Standards, Writing the BCP, Responsibilities of the Corporate Continuity Planner, Working with Local Authorities, Building (Business Process) Teams (The Delphi Method), Building a Corporate Team and Demonstrating Team Effort, Participants, Scenarios, Rules, Facilitator Leading Questions, Evaluation, Common Findings, Other Matters, Conclusion and Summary, Question and Answers, Case Studies

Chapter 6 83
Business Ethics: An Oxymoron?
Moral Standards, Recognizing Moral Impact, Ethical Duties, Moral Analysis and Economic Outcomes, The Moral Basis of Economic Theory, The Moral Objections to Economic Theory, The Moral Claims of Economic Theory: Effectiveness, Pragmatic Objections to Economic Theory, Moral Analysis and Legal Requirements, Reward System, Ethics Committee, Judiciary Board, Employee Training in Ethics, Moral Analysis and Ethical Duties, the Principle of Utilitarian Benefits, the Principle of Universal Duties, the Principle of Distributive Justice, the Principle of Contributive Liberty, Trust, Commitment, and Other Factors, A Business Organization Should Be Moral, Consistency: Aligning Corporate Social Responsibility with the Business Plan, Ethical Challenges in Human Resources, An Aristotelian Take on Business Ethics, Aristotelian Questions for Corporate Leaders, The Distribution of Rewards in Organizations,

Examples of Aristotelian Business
Leadership, Sexual Harassment, Conclusion

Bibliography *101*

About the Author *105*

Chapter 1

Some Tidbits

Introduction
The modern business world is volatile; therefore, change is inevitable! Appropriate plans should be drawn up to combat and master the effects of change. Communication between employees who have been selected on the basis of merit, i.e., qualifications, experience, character (otherwise, they may disrespect and cheat you), personality traits, and (corporate) cultural fit *rather than favoritism*, together with persuasion and adequate training, will help eliminate resistance to change while promoting corporate success.

Effective Leadership: A Torch Which Must Be Passed On!
Leadership is the art of mobilizing others toward shared aspirations. In a business enterprise, management is responsible for taking care of employees who, in turn, are responsible for taking care of customers, stakeholders, and related outside parties, such as the government and the community, in an ethical manner. This approach also considers implications for the environment and results in profitable growth combined with an increase in the welfare of all parties involved.

Great leaders are visionaries whose intuition helps them to recognize and capitalize on business opportunities in a timely manner. Their success is based on surrounding themselves with "like-minded" professionals who complement them to help reinforce their strengths and eliminate their weaknesses. They build teams consisting of individuals who complement one another in a way that ensures consistent performance in line with corporate goals. The mantra embodied herein is "Build grand castles in the air while ensuring that they rest on solid foundations." This is in direct contrast to mediocre leaders who surround themselves with yes-people who, by their very nature, are unable to contribute positively to the bottom line!

The wisdom of effective leaders enables them to appreciate the views of their inner circle and others. In situations where consensus cannot be reached, they have an uncanny ability to cut to the chase and make informed decisions. They foster an environment that encourages the sharing of ideas through brainstorming while realizing that innovation need not be preceded by the existence of committees.

True leaders place a great deal of emphasis on culture and shared values. They realize that business involves human beings and that profitable growth results from fruitful relationships. They normally possess both formal and informal power. Formal power is entrusted to them by virtue of their position in the company. Informal power results from their core belief system. They lead by example, thus earning the respect and admiration of their peers and subordinates. As a result, employees are enthusiastic about going beyond the call of duty for "their" leaders.

Great leaders build organizations that are vibrant and performance-driven. They structure employee compensation packages in a way that promotes and reinforces the right behaviors and rewards people on the basis of individual as well as team performance. They believe that a base salary pays the bills, whereas variable compensation, including earnings before interest, taxes, dividends and amortization (EBITDA)-based bonuses, motivates employees to challenge themselves and increase their contribution to the firm on a consistent basis. These leaders find reasons to pay bonuses as opposed to those leaders who find reasons to deprive employees of bonuses they truly deserve!

Leadership traits can create a virtuous cycle for the firm's management, employees, clients, stakeholders, and others. Great leaders have a natural flair. There are those who believe that their effectiveness can be increased through education, other methods of training and development, and experience, though to a limited extent.

Interviewing

Interviews should be planned in terms of structure and approach and conducted in a professional manner. The climate should be appropriate; the process should be controlled and documented with both interviewer and interviewee knowing how to probe. A telephone interview acts as a screening process, which should precede reference checks, and the latter should precede a face-to-face interview to help eliminate any "undesirable candidates" from the pool of interviewees. *Candidates for a job should be selected on the basis of merit and the precise job requirements rather than on the basis of friendship, relationships, or any other irrelevant criteria!*

Appraisal interviews are meant to improve the performance of employees and the organization itself through communication, feedback, and subsequent action. These interviews should be regular and frequent (say, quarterly), as opposed to being conducted annually, where the focus is on "salary" increase rather than on performance, scope for improvement, and contribution to the bottom line. Counseling interviews are aimed at relieving stress and improving behavior, as well as performance. These interviews usually take place as and when the need arises.

Listening

Listening is fundamental to communication and successful business operations and includes observing tone of voice and body language and concentrating on the gist of what is being said.

Mentoring
Mentoring involves the formation of relationships between senior and junior employees to facilitate training, career development, emotional support, and stress relief.

Motivation
In order to spur employees to desirable performance, they must be motivated through an ongoing process of respect, recognition, monetary and health benefits, time off, and other incentives.

Conflict Management

Conflict arises as a result of the interaction between different parties: employees, prospects, customers, suppliers, community, government, human nature, policies, procedures, and limited resources (people, time, money, and equipment). Conflicts should be addressed effectively, rather than in an unduly aggressive manner. The objective is to solve the problem amicably, instead of engaging in mere target practice!

Conflicts can lead to better decisions while stimulating and promoting creativity, following a thorough understanding of the problem(s) at hand. Effective resolution of conflicts can lead to increased respect between the conflicting parties, thus boosting corporate performance.

Consultants

Business is becoming increasingly complex; hence, the need for a consultant from time to time. A consultant is an independent professional who uses his/her expertise in general management, business development, business ethics, accounting, law, engineering, health, public relations, marketing, or other areas to solve a client's problems in return for a fee.

The firm should review its existing pool of talent, compare the (actual plus opportunity) costs of training an existing employee with the pros and cons of hiring an independent consultant, and

1. identify needs and ascertain whether they can be met internally—failing which, independent consultants should be interviewed to obtain their testimonials, proposals, and related fees;
2. establish the client-consultant relationship through mutual respect, trust, integrity, cooperation, and a sound work ethic, which promotes improved corporate performance—the written contract must specify the responsibilities of the firm and the hired consultant;
3. beware of consultants who provide generic solutions or who cause their clients to be dependent on them long after completion of the project; and
4. maximize the *difference* between revenues and costs instead of merely minimizing costs.

Customers

The existence of a business organization is largely dependent upon a satisfied customer base and a motivated workforce. As the saying goes, "If you do not take care of your customers, somebody else will!" *Keeping the customer satisfied is not enough—customers should love your enterprise, as explained in the book,* Raving Fans, *by Ken Blanchard and Sheldon Bowles!* Therefore, the organization should hire and retain the right people and motivate them through fairness, respect, communication, recognition, rewards, and the setting of realistic standards and responsibilities. Continuous feedback from customers helps monitor and improve results.

Delegation

Delegation frees up time of the delegator and enables training and motivation via a transfer of responsibilities. The delegator and the party being delegated to must understand and appreciate the task(s) being delegated. Moreover, the delegator should trust and empower the party to whom the task is being delegated and should ensure that he/she has the ability to perform as required while offering help where necessary. Improper delegation causes chaos and increases stress!

Employees should be fully aware of what is expected of them in terms of behavior in the workplace. The rules of the business organization should be current, fair, precise, as comprehensive as possible, framed in writing, and communicated in clear terms by qualified personnel. Organizations should be aware of legal constraints and employees' rights of appeal.

Employee orientation should explain the rules (as documented in the employee manual), the reasons for their existence, and the consequences of violation. When there is a violation, the guilty party should be spoken to, in a polite and diplomatic manner, to explain why the rule exists and how its violation affects the company. If the violation continues, there must be an oral or written warning depending on the severity of the infringement. Subsequent infractions may lead to suspension, followed by termination, subject to the employee's legal rights.

Rights of Appeal

A system that calls for discipline should be accompanied by a system of appeal, e.g., the human resources department, to listen to both sides of the story and to solve problems in a fair manner, thus, preventing managers and other employees from flaunting or abusing their powers.

Diversity in Organizations

Employees differ in terms of sex, race, ethnicity, age, sexual orientation, and physical ability, to say the least. Older workers may benefit the organization because of their extensive experience, despite being set in their ways, and you should bear the foregoing in mind when managing them.

Organizations that value diversity attract talented employees and minimize communication gaps due to language or other barriers. Adapting to people of different cultures, backgrounds, and perspectives contributes to improved performance. Failure of any given individual does not imply failure of any given category—e.g., women, gay individuals, or people of color.

Unfortunately, many business organizations discriminate against individuals of foreign origin while claiming that they are open to employing people of different cultural backgrounds! This is unethical and contrary to desirable business practice! Then the press and television newscasters inform everyone that "there is a shortage of professionals" in the country!

Intercultural Communication

The workplace calls for knowledge of different cultures, customs, etiquette, nuances, and methods of communication to help deal with individuals of different backgrounds as listed below:

1. *Greetings.* In some countries, people are addressed by their last name and greeted with a handshake, a kiss on the cheek, or a bow. There are different ways of shaking hands or bowing. What is acceptable for men may not necessarily be acceptable for women.
2. *Dining Etiquette.* One may be expected to eat different food or food served from a common dish or in a certain manner. Refusal may result in a loss of business.
3. *Gift Giving.* Beware of the nature and timing of the gifts in question.
4. *Dress and Appearance.* This should normally be smart but conservative; certain colors are unacceptable in some countries. Shoes may need to be removed in certain areas.
5. *Time Consciousness.* In some countries, keeping strict time schedules may be considered as being impatient and aggressive rather than organized and disciplined.
6. *Language and Communication.* This includes posture, gestures, and eye contact. The national language is always important. Being direct may be regarded as being impolite.

7. *Work Attitudes and Other Variables.* Attitudes toward work and leisure, loyalty, respect, and the motivational value of money are important factors.

Employee Assistance Programs (EAPs)

Employee assistance programs must solve performance-related problems through identification and guidance. Organizations face substantial costs for impaired employees in terms of higher rates of sick leave, accidents, workers' compensation, the hidden costs of poor decisions, morale of coworkers, threats to public safety, corporate theft, turnover, and training of new employees.

Special Needs/Mentally or Physically Challenged Individuals

Some employees need counseling. Dual-career couples may need flexible hours or child-care benefits. Mentally or physically challenged employees may need specialized equipment, interpreters, and appropriate adjustments in their job functions or work schedules; otherwise, they cannot be dismissed for substandard performance.

AIDS

Victims of Acquired Immune Deficiency Syndrome (AIDS), Human Immune Deficiency Virus (HIV), Severe Acute Respiratory Syndrome (SARS), and other diseases may be regarded as disabled with legislation to protect them, but should not be allowed to harm the bottom line.

Substance Abuse

Everyone should be aware of the effects of substance abuse, the costs associated with it and the possible remedies.

Organizational Policies

Organizations must obtain guidance and advice prior to formulating policies to address issues related to hiring, retention, dismissal, education, benefits, confidentiality, assistance, guidance, counseling, and other matters. Employees should be educated regarding disabilities, preventive measures, and implications for welfare. Medical records should be kept confidential so that non-AIDS sufferers are not in a position to know which employees are suffering from AIDS. *Firms often try to cut costs by replacing higher-paid employees with lower-paid employees without a detailed analysis of the implications in the medium-and long-term, i.e., managers are often shortsighted. (Also see Management: Flirting with Disaster! from RoseDog books.)*

Ethics

Ethics is defined by *The Concise Oxford Dictionary* as "the science of morals in human conduct." There is more to ethics than merely sending e-mail messages regarding the importance of ethics, convening meetings, and signing memos of agreement! *Ethical behavior must exist at all levels and in all circumstances*, including when reviewing salaries, promotions, implementing decision-making styles, communication practices, and policies.

The code of ethics must be discussed with *all* employees, with feedback and review, through meetings, questionnaires, and training sessions in order to promote effectiveness within a moral environment. There must be recognition and rewards for observance of the code of ethics.

Family-Friendly Management

Female managers often ensure that firms accommodate the personal needs of employees, including care of the elderly and (reasonable) personal usage of business equipment, e.g., the telephone. With men playing a greater role in running the family, the family-friendly style also helps them and results in lower absenteeism and higher productivity through reduced stress.

Family-friendly options include the following:
1. Allowances toward child care, afterschool care, summer camps, and elderly care
2. Flexible hours of work to accommodate personal needs
3. Work-life programs to assist employees with work and family conflicts, counseling, stress, time management, communication strategies, exercise, and nutrition programs

Feedback

Feedback and subsequent action promotes improved performance and should
1. be precise and ongoing, at the appropriate time and place, thus letting people know what is expected of them and promoting corporate effectiveness;
2. build trust and understanding while strengthening relationships; and
3. reduce customer and employee stress and discontent via frequent opinion surveys.

Innovation and Creativity

Leaders must be logical, intuitive, diplomatic, and innovative—i.e., they must introduce policies, procedures, and practices that do not hinder creativity while simplifying work and providing job enrichment. Creative individuals normally exhibit a considerable degree of self-confidence, curiosity, and a tendency to take risks—i.e., they are adventurous!

Negotiation
Negotiation involves a meeting of the minds through an exchange of information and possible compromise, resulting (hopefully) in a win-win situation for all parties concerned.

Networking
Managers must network with different parties, thus developing fruitful relationships based on "the law of comparative advantage," as discussed in basic textbooks on economics.

Organizational Culture
Organizational culture is shaped by and communicated through the behavior of leaders of the organization and is reflected in policies—e.g., hiring, promotions and termination policies, procedures and methods, decision making, and operations. This culture influences performance.

Orientation of New Employees
Employee orientation helps ease new employees into the organization by informing them regarding its nature, history, structure, mission, philosophy, goals, and the precise roles and responsibilities of both parties. This reduces the initial stress/tension faced by new employees.

Politics in Organizations
In order to be promoted and to gain power based on one's ideas, views, and the support of fellow employees, one must find a way to be accepted and liked in an organization. The

approach should be subtle in some cases and up front in others. By being patient, cautious, and observing, one can learn to express oneself and build relationships through careful negotiation.

Public Relations

Public relations can enhance the corporate image and promote success via communication with insiders and outsiders—unions, customers, suppliers, press, government, and public. The organization should also sponsor activities for the less fortunate and donate to charities.

Sexual Harassment

Sexual harassment is defined as an unwelcome sexual advance and includes body language, e.g., gestures, that make individuals stray from corporate objectives. Most cases of sexual harassment involve a man harassing a woman and may not be reported because the victim may be accused of inviting the same, overreacting to a compliment, trying to draw attention to herself, or there may be adverse repercussions on/off the job, including embarrassment. It is difficult to establish a clear link between sexual harassment and organizational expenses, decreased morale, productivity, or high employee turnover. In order to eliminate sexual harassment and related problems, there must be
1. a policy statement defining sexual harassment and stressing zero tolerance of the same;

2. training to provide guidance on how to avoid sexual harassment;
3. reporting and investigative procedures to understand and eliminate sexual harassment; and
4. disciplinary procedures based on the law, company rules, and the facts in question.

Stress Management

Stress may result from financial, emotional, psychological, sexual, or other problems. Stress should be managed; otherwise, it may lead to conflicts, absenteeism, high employee turnover, and lower productivity. Good nutrition, sound exercise programs, and leisure activities will certainly reduce stress. Family and friends may alleviate or add to stress. The degree of stress is high in certain occupations—police officers, firefighters, doctors, engineers, teachers, and others. The work environment, organizational culture and philosophy, policies, procedures, work relationships, noise, poor heating/cooling and lighting, improper hygiene conditions, insufficient medical and other benefits, inadequate training, lack of sufficient challenge in a job, unreasonable deadlines, or the need for recognition and improvement may also add to stress.

Teamwork

The business enterprise would benefit greatly from teamwork, brainstorming, and participative leadership. The team must operate within an environment that fosters openness and trust. Conflicts should be handled with tact while avoiding hostility.

Many years ago, management told workers what to do and showed them how to do it; workers proceeded without any questions or feedback! Today, it is not feasible for information to be centralized in the hands of management. Peter Drucker stated, "Now we are managing people who are paid for their knowledge. We have never done that, and we don't know how to do it."

Although people have worked together for centuries, the formal concept of teams was popularized in America, in the 1960s and thereafter, with the Quality Circle (QC) concept (as explained in chapter 2.) Hewlett-Packard and Xerox introduced the QC concept in their manufacturing and other departments in the 1970s.

Initially, managers resisted QCs because they did not like sharing information and control with employees and being considered "weak" leaders. Since then, management has realized that good teams require good managers who coach rather than command, value employees' opinions (including challenging assumptions and methods), and reward them for their contribution, thereby boosting morale, employee satisfaction, and profits. Teams are effective when individual expectations are integrated with team goals as outlined below:

1. Blue Cross Blue Shield of Florida saw a 32.5 percent increase in productivity and a 19 percent decrease in cost per claim when a team ensured that the appropriate processes and procedures were implemented to exceed the standards established by the state of Florida.
2. Lucent Technologies enjoyed cost savings of approximately $2 million after a team helped to improve factory yield for its electronic circuit assembly process.
3. Solectron saw a 50 percent improvement in machine

utilization and defect generation resulting in cost savings when a team implemented a quality improvement process.

Total Quality Management (TQM)
TQM measures the costs for reworking, replacing, modifying, handling of complaints, and loss of customer referrals and goodwill resulting from defects in products/services and involves a systematic team effort to continuously improve processes, quality, and customer satisfaction. It takes years to create a sound TQM; therefore, short-term results are out of the question!

Credit for Japan's quality control standards and reputation goes mainly to W. Edwards Deming (who was influenced by Professor Genichi Taguchi, Japan's quality management expert), a former professor of statistics at New York University, who urged companies *to focus on continuous improvements and doing things right the first time around through a process of recording defects, understanding what happened, instituting changes, and noting improvements in quality until the job was done right!* Deming was invited to Japan to conduct a seminar for businessmen in 1950, and he shifted the emphasis from maximizing profits to creating high-quality products!

Professor Kaoru Ishikawa, who introduced the concept of QCs in 1962, is also associated with the companywide quality control movement that started in Japan in the 1950s following the visits of Deming and Juran. All employees study statistical methods and participate in quality control, which includes quality of product, aftersales service, management, the company itself, and its stakeholders and is subject to internal and external quality control audits.

TQM was a good fit for Japan's culture and its need to rebuild its economy after the Second World War. In the United States, however, firms were still influenced by the management theories of Frederick W. Taylor (1856-1915), who believed that managers were responsible for ensuring that workers performed their tasks at specified rates of efficiency based on the division of labor into small repetitive tasks and related time-and-motion studies. TQM would require fundamental changes in company culture—flattening hierarchies and dispersing responsibility. Nevertheless, when faced with the dominance of Japanese companies in their markets, several American and European companies adopted Deming's methods in the late 1970s.

In the 1980s, billions of dollars were invested in training, consulting, and management education efforts in an all-out effort to close the quality gap between the United States and Japan. In 1987, US Congress created a national quality award competition, named in honor of Commerce Secretary Malcolm Baldrige, to promote quality and corporate effectiveness, with major changes in 1997. *The adoption of TQM principles is now global and extends beyond manufacturing.*

Termination of Employees and Restrictions

Before dismissing an employee, managers should be aware of legal implications, the impact on goodwill, the financial and psychological impact on the employee concerned, possible assistance, and the effect on existing employees in terms of emotions and the burden of extra work. If a letter of recommendation is given to the departing employee, it should be carefully worded.

Training

In a volatile business environment, continuous training and adjustment motivates employees through increased knowledge and improved performance, respect, recognition, and due rewards. Effective training minimizes the "skills" gap—i.e., the gap between knowledge needed for effectiveness and that actually possessed by employees. Effective training will yield improvements of near infinite proportions. The Kirkpatrick model is used by several business enterprises and suggests that training should be measured at four levels:

Level 1: Reaction—Did the participants like the program?

Level 2: Learning—What knowledge, skills, and other benefits did the participants gain?

Level 3: Behavior—Do the participants behave differently as a result of the program?

Level 4: Results—Did the program reduce costs, improve productivity, and the quality of work?

While it is difficult to quantify the precise results emanating from training, employees should be continuously monitored for performance and feedback. Training sessions must suit the precise requirements of the firm in question after weighing the actual costs, such as amounts paid to the provider of the training and facilities used (i.e., room, heating, lighting, printing, refreshments, beverages), and the opportunity costs, such as the cost of time spent away from the job and its impact on the bottom line, wastage due to poor quality training, training of the wrong people or inadequate training facilities, including the training environment. The foregoing costs should be compared with the benefits generated by the training. The approach should be flexible enough to be adjusted within a volatile business environment.

Employee Turnover

High employee turnover is an indication of employee dissatisfaction and a reflection of inadequate management skills resulting in high costs of lost knowledge, the need for retraining, *and the added frustration of extra work for existing employees.* Regular turnover provides an injection of new blood, skills, and experience, but there are costs as discussed above. Other reasons for employee turnover include the following: marriage, childbearing, relocation of a spouse, illness, family problems, need for financial independence, the need to return to school, options for early retirement, and so on. Therefore, firms should examine recruitment, placement, and promotion procedures, appraisals, and rewards and leadership styles and encourage continuous feedback.

Violence in the Workplace

This includes verbal and physical abuse and can result in significant losses, in terms of money and reputation, unless monitored and controlled. There should be adequate preemployment screening procedures—e.g., screening (telephone) interview, checking employment references, credit history, and criminal records. Managers should know how to diffuse anger and how to deal with inappropriate conduct at work. Employees should be trained in "violence management."

Virtual Management

A virtual team consists of a group of individuals who work together but rarely meet because they operate from different locations. A virtual manager is someone who manages people from a distance with minimum face-to-face contact; therefore, trust is very important. Technology helps to fill the vacuum, but there are possibilities for misunderstandings. Virtual managers must possess certain skills:

1. *Effective Communication and Interpretation.* In the absence of face-to-face contact, one cannot interpret body language and needs sound communication skills and appropriate processes, mediums, and systems to monitor team effort. Since the wording of e-mail messages is usually informal, one should not be oversensitive when reading and interpreting such messages.
2. *Interpersonal Skills.* Virtual management calls for excellent interpersonal skills and a thorough understanding of individual differences, motivations, values, the contexts people work in, as well as "an understanding of who can do what." The team members must feel respected and cared for.
3. *Trust.* Trust enables fruitful communication and delegation, leading to improved performance.
4. *Team Effort.* Virtual team members must be proactive while operating with little supervision. The roles and expectations of virtual managers should be spelled out to the team members.
5. *Results-Oriented Approach.* Focus on results rather than hours worked.

6. *Organizational Goals.* Virtual managers must ensure that their team members understand the link between their performance and the overall goals of the business enterprise.

Conclusion and Summary

We have reviewed several concepts in management in an attempt to draw one's attention to the main areas of business. Other areas including Japanese management, trade unions, women at work, business continuity planning, and business ethics will be covered in subsequent chapters.

Chapter 2

Japanese Management: For Better, for Worse

Following the second World War, Japan was faced with the daunting task of having to rebuild its economy. There were serious problems associated with low production levels, unemployment, inflation, and a shortage of housing facilities. The Japanese responded by focusing on capital-intensive methods of production, employee bonuses based on profitability, and a strong emphasis on technological advance while simplifying their assembly process.

The Japanese Economic Miracle

Japan has an extremely high literacy rate with a university degree being a prerequisite for entry into the managerial field. Most students have advanced degrees and training.

The vast improvement in health standards has resulted in a healthier, more energetic, and more productive workforce with a lower rate of absenteeism. However, increased life expectancy and the declining birthrate put pressure on the ageing population to perform in the workplace.

Lifetime Employment

Lifetime employment, which was a common trend until the 1990s, implied working until "normal" retirement for men or until marriage for women. Former employees could be re-employed on a part-time or temporary basis and laid off during a recession to reduce labor costs. *Salaries and promotions used to be based on seniority and the team approach rather than on results.* Lifetime employment was successful in Japan because of a familylike environment, lifetime training, improved performance, and standards being reviewed frequently.

Unfavorable economic conditions in the 1990s led to employees being laid off or being assigned less-challenging tasks, thereby causing boredom and eventual substandard performance or resignation throughout Japan. Moreover, the younger generation is more career-minded than its predecessors, with a tendency to switch jobs often, thus providing a new challenge for managers.

Americans introduced many great ideas in Japan, and the Japanese applied them fully—e.g., Deming's quality control methods and the zero defects principle. The view underlying these concepts is that absolute perfection is unattainable, but improvements are always possible! Employees are continuously motivated to improve their performance while being trained in the functions of related jobs. Teamwork and trust are more important than bypassing the system for immediate results based on initiative!

The Godfather System

The godfather system calls for young executives to be (informally) attached to a senior executive who monitors progress and ensures the employee's steady development. Employees are carefully selected and required to attend a weekly training program, which covers the work of the department rather than the job of any given individual. This develops team spirit and promotes a better understanding of the *Zen* philosophy of education, which focuses on performance and the introduction of new tools, processes, and methods. The *Confucian* philosophy of training, on the other hand, focuses on a new job and higher status.

Is Japan One Big Firm?

Government, business, and family are closely knit in Japan largely because
1. the Japanese consider almost every question from the national point of view;
2. the Japanese, being very diplomatic, have developed the art of making conflicts (between owners, managers, employees, customers, and others) constructive;
3. the strong urge to achieve *ringi* (consensus) prompts most Japanese managers to remain in touch with all major groups—executives, government officials, and others—to help understand their views, expectations, hopes, and anxieties through endless discussions.

Lessons to be Learned from the Japanese
1. The Japanese place a great deal of emphasis on national welfare.
2. Close attention is paid to the selection, placement, training, and development of all employees. Managers demand improved performance from employees continuously and will fight tooth and nail to keep good employees. Managers maintain a steady relationship with schools to ensure a continuous supply of young graduates for recruitment.
3. Decision making is on a group consensus basis where egos are set aside and the mistakes formerly made by experienced people are avoided. The obsolete is discarded immediately.
4. Employers design welfare measures to suit employees, e.g., dowry for unmarried women.
5. There are short- and long-term budgets, e.g., for the research and development department.
6. Marketing strategy addresses the specific requirements of the various world markets.

Some Perplexities in Japan
The increase in life expectancy, combined with the fall in birthrate, has resulted in a shortage of labor and a decline in productivity despite the introduction of machines, which incorporate advanced technology, and the induction of women and foreigners into the workforce. Women normally prefer to work on a part-time basis because they dislike harsh competition and are not as mobile as men. As a result, few women become managers. The Japanese Equal Employment Opportunity Law has led firms to categorize female job applicants as *sogoshoku* (a career track job seeker) or *ippanshoku* (a seeker of general office work).

The younger and more highly educated generation believes in a more balanced life rather than a "work is life" approach, with promotion based on performance rather than seniority! The demand for higher education has led to severe competition for admission and soaring fees at educational establishments. The resulting stress has led to a higher suicide rate. Whereas university graduates find it difficult to obtain suitable jobs, non-graduates are considered mainly for manual jobs. The demand for manual workers exceeds the supply of such workers; therefore, their wages rise at a faster rate than the wages of educated workers!

With the increasing cost of food and education (the basics of Japanese society), the real income of the Japanese family is on the decline. Peter Drucker suggests the following:
1. An extension of the retirement age and retraining of redundant workers
2. Modification of the seniority-based wage and promotion system
3. Reduction of domestic prices and the use of cheap labor and advanced technology

Industrial Relations in Japan

Japan seems to have resolved the perennial conflict between workers' and owners' interests—mainly because their relationship is based on moral, rather than contractual, concerns. Trade unions fight management rather than the business enterprise in an attempt to increase the size of the pie and their respective shares in the larger pie! Where labor is expensive, the Japanese may subcontract to newly industrialized countries such as Korea, Taiwan, and Hong Kong.

Lack of precision is often regarded as a virtue; case-to-case interpretation is encouraged via vague regulations. Emphasis is placed on *wa*—i.e., harmony, politeness, respect, discipline, punctuality, patience, persistence, a good relationship, gift-giving, gestures, and body language—rather than on results! Decisions are based on the *ringi* system, i.e., group consensus. The focus on mistakes, rather than accomplishments, results in a conservative approach to decision making.

Quality: An Overall Emphasis

Quality, cost, delivery, and service are of paramount importance in Japan. Japanese standards are generally far more stringent than international standards. Moreover, when dealing with a Japanese businessman, one deals with his group; facades, loyalty, solidarity, and Japanese culture and customs are important. Therefore, a go-between, coupled with research, pilot projects, and an approach that reflects courtesy are advisable before plunging into the Japanese market.

The Japanese believe that neatness promotes efficiency. Therefore, Japanese businessmen like to meet with the engineers who have developed a product and to observe the manufacturing process and the inventory control methods. The just-in-time (JIT) method of inventory control was introduced by the Japanese in an attempt to reduce the costs of holding and managing inventory. The Japanese believe in easy access to suppliers with implications for shorter lead times, i.e., the time spent between placing an order and receiving the items in question.

Japanese customers will not switch suppliers on the basis of price alone because they risk losing the benefits of a long-term relationship and facing the consequences of dealing with an unknown supplier. There is trust between customer and supplier, with both parties being aware of market conditions. Likewise, Japanese suppliers feel a sense of loyalty toward their customers—e.g., Sony's initial reluctance to discontinue Betamax videocassettes after the initial success of VHS videocassettes. A replacement or refund may be offered to dissatisfied customers.

The person who offers *shidoh* (guidance) to subordinates or distributors ensures that the *shidoh* is taken advantage of. *Shinrai* (trust) is fundamental to all relationships and implies following the agreement and generally accepted business behavior, with disputes being resolved through discussion and compromise rather than litigation. The person who introduces someone to a third party is often held responsible for any misunderstanding that ensues.

In Japan, competition is intense and prices tumble fast; despite which, the Japanese do not display a tendency to discredit their competitors. Moreover, Japanese businessmen usually prefer local products to foreign ones, regardless of price, and prefer to invest in the development of technology instead of buying the same because they wish to maintain full control of their operations rather than be at the "mercy" of outsiders.

The system keeps track of each individual, thus preventing him/her from doing wrong and disappearing! For information on finance and local contacts, consult the Japan External Trade Organization (JETRO)—an arm of the Ministry of International Trade and Industry (MITI).

In order to understand how the Japanese operate, one must be aware of the following matters:

1. *Group orientation.* The Japanese believe that there is strength in unity. Accordingly, the welfare of the group takes precedence over the welfare of any given individual! Employees are encouraged to follow the leader rather than to display initiative. The new generation is more individualistic, assertive, and changes jobs more frequently than its predecessors. When introduced, a Japanese individual will normally mention

which group he/she belongs to and then disclose his/her name. The open office plan promotes the group feeling by encouraging employees to communicate freely with one another as team members.

Most Japanese employers are reluctant to hire (experienced) employees in mid-career for fear that they may have difficulty fitting in with existing employees, and being loyal to the firm as well!

The contract of employment used to be considered a commitment for life! Hence, there were often too many employees. Recessionary pressures have led firms to restructure and downsize in order to compete. Fringe benefits, such as medical coverage and membership in sports/recreational clubs, may be offered to employees to help develop the family feeling.

Information sharing is duly emphasized where beneficial to the organization. Managers are encouraged to analyze corporate problems and to propose feasible solutions.

The Quality Circle (QC) concept was introduced in Japan in April 1962 by Dr. Kaoru Ishikawa (although some people insist that the concept was introduced in the US Army after 1945). This concept, whereby groups of employees voluntarily participate in discussions and problem solving, thus motivating them through increased responsibility, has been adopted in most parts of the world as a morale booster, emphasizing employee involvement.

A QC consists of several individuals performing the same functions/tasks, who voluntarily agree to form a team to (1) discuss job-related problems through brainstorming, open communication, and a positive consensus-based approach; and (2) propose

solutions with management support, i.e., participative management. QCs improve corporate results if
a. members of the QC are effective in their jobs and in QC techniques, and the team leader is a skilled coach rather than a commander (with or without a budget); and
b. managers are trained in QC techniques, encourage the formation and operation of QCs, accept QC decisions based on consensus without any fear of loss of power (resulting from sharing of authority), and are patient—i.e., they do not emphasize short-term gains!

Several years ago, management told workers what to do and showed them how to do it, and workers did the job without any feedback! Today, it is not feasible for information to be centralized in the hands of management! Drucker stated, "Now we are managing people who are paid for their knowledge. We have never done that, and we don't know how to do it."

The *zero defects* program motivates employees toward a specific goal: zero defect, improved quality, and higher profits through increased competitive strength. Harmony or *wa* is stressed at all times in business and personal life. There has been a trend toward a more direct approach when expressing opinions, and this may cause problems for *wa*.

2. *Diligence.* The Japanese have an insatiable thirst for knowledge. Employers sponsor self-improvement courses on the job and at universities throughout the world. They spend about 10 percent of sales revenue on training and development with expectations of multiple dividends!

Most Japanese employees are conscientious and effective when given responsibility for specific results and the freedom to adopt suitable methods without undue interference.

3. *Aesthetics and perfectionism.* Japanese people appreciate natural (and other) beauty. The Japanese always stress the importance of neatness, organization, and discipline, plus the need for safety in the workplace, thus facilitating high quality and productivity.

A shorter working week may adversely affect the Japanese quest for perfection! Employees are faced with a dilemma: if they spend time with their families while their colleagues are at work, they are "preventing successful teamwork and harmony." Also, they have become dependent on overtime income, although many employers tend to refuse overtime pay.

4. *Curiosity and emphasis on innovation.* The Japanese tend to be receptive to new information of how their foreign counterparts operate. Firms will often send their representatives to exhibitions and trade shows to gain an insight into new developments. The Japanese are extremely keen on continuous improvement. Most firms have a "new business development" department, which conducts research on a continuous basis and is aware of products and services that can complement the existing (product and service) lines of the firm and satisfy the volatile demand of customers and prospects. The Japanese believe in *kaizen* (every method can be improved to the point of perfection).

5. *Respect for form* and hana yori dango (rewards before recognition). The Japanese follow certain customs and traditions. When businessmen are introduced, they bow and then exchange cards. Japanese people bow in different ways: fifteen degrees for simple greetings, thirty degrees when giving thanks,

and forty-five degrees when apologizing. They pay attention to titles and rank in the organization. Most Japanese business enterprises have a dress code: normally, conservative for office employees, with uniforms for women and factory personnel.

New employees are welcomed on a group basis; the orientation may include plunging into a river in mere underwear as a method of "purification from old habits and ways of thinking."

In many companies, all employees meet at the start of every working day to discuss concerns. Seating arrangements at meetings and the common room are meant to reflect respect for seniors, supervisors, customers, and others even at informal gatherings. Often, the organization will stress the importance of certain issues, e.g., workplace safety or customer satisfaction, and all employees will strive to achieve the desired results. Japanese employees are firm believers in *hana yori dango*.

6. *Competition and rewards.* The Japanese love to compete and increase market share continuously—they are not satisfied with increasing short-term profits alone! Most companies focus on satisfying their employees and customers en route to increased profitability. They believe in capital investment, new technologies, being cost effective, quality conscious, developing new lines of business, and diversifying, but not through mergers or acquisitions (with resulting changes in ownership, management, and some loss of jobs).

7. *Silence is golden.* The Japanese are generally good listeners. They are becoming more eloquent but do not respect people who talk too much. They take brief notes during meetings and proceed to ask

questions if the notes are difficult to follow. Many firms do not have precise policies, procedures, or job descriptions—the latter are believed to hinder progress and flexibility. Perhaps the Japanese need to be precise, logical, articulate (in the English language), outspoken, and open to criticism from non-Japanese.

8. *Time is money.* The Japanese are a group of highly disciplined and punctual individuals who realize that time is money. They believe in being on schedule as far as appointments, delivery schedules, and other matters are concerned.

Japanese production cycles are usually shorter, and product development is usually faster than in most parts of the world—e.g., in the auto industry, new models are developed within three years, whereas their American and European counterparts normally do so in five or more years. However, US and European businessmen seem to be faster in setting up new businesses.

Conclusion

The Japanese style of management has several pointers, which the rest of the world should be aware of, in order to improve the bottom line. Perhaps Japanese managers and other employees should be more precise and bottom-line oriented.

Chapter 3

Trade Unions: A Necessary Evil?

Before discussing the nature of trade unions, one must review the role of human beings in a firm.

In order to run a business, one needs people, money, and time. Since no individual can corner the market on all aspects of business, managers must employ people to help improve the bottom line. Unlike robots, human beings have feelings and are selfish in nature. Therefore, employees should be selected on the basis of merit and duly motivated (to focus on corporate rather than personal goals), or else they will resign in terms of their attitude on the job or physically, with implications for employee turnover, costs of training, mistakes, and re-establishing relationships.

Freud believed that man was basically aggressive, lustful, and unscrupulous. Maslow challenged this view, contending that human needs form a hierarchy—they form a pyramid, with physical needs (e.g., air, water, food, shelter, and sleep) at the base, followed by safety needs, love needs, esteem needs, self-realization (to perform at maximum potential), beauty (to look his or her best and be appreciated for the same), and knowledge (and perfection) at the apex. Only when a human being satisfies one level of need will he or she move to the next level of needs!

One cannot assume that individuals are objective and rational because people see "what they want to see" based on perceptual frameworks and experience—i.e., they perceive data based on their values, backgrounds, experiences, biases, personalities, and goals rather than the facts!

Objectives of the Business Enterprise

Firms aim to serve their stakeholders, employees, customers, suppliers, government, and general public. The resulting compromise, due to conflicts of interest, leaves a residue of profit, which firms aim to satisfice rather than maximize in the face of numerous practical considerations. Objectives include the following: growth, innovation, favorable image and goodwill, liquidity, percentage market share, reasonable safety margin, conservative financing, and effectiveness and reasonable compensation packages. Decisions may reflect the views of several participants.

Management should focus on effectiveness through teamwork, motivation, and goal congruence.

In the real world, people are busy partly because they do not review and simplify methods and processes—e.g., computer programs can be made more comprehensive, input methods can be simplified and computer-generated reports can avoid duplicated or unnecessary information.

Developing a Relationship with Freelancers

Freelancers help avoid the burden of a salary and complications related to employee rights; there must be a good fit between the firm and the freelancer in terms of ability and relevant experience. The written contract should specify (precisely) the duties of both parties—e.g., the assignment, responsibilities, compensation and payment schedule, and operational guidelines such as teamwork, info to be imparted, communication channels, dissatisfaction with the service and other matters.

Owners and employees often believe that they have conflicting interests—they feel that the gain of one party represents a loss to the other! Both parties should state their interests in precise terms, thereby setting a foundation for successful negotiation and conflict resolution while considering separate and common interests. This will minimize labor disputes and strikes.

Teamwork and employee participation in decision making give employees a sense of belonging; different perspectives contribute to better decisions. However, it is difficult to alter the selfish nature of human beings and the resulting conflicts geared toward "a bigger slice of the existing pie" rather than the overall welfare of the company and its associates. Hence, motivation, negotiation, and conflict resolution skills resulting in a win-win situation are of paramount importance.

A Labor Union

A labor union consists of employees who have combined to increase bargaining power and negotiate with their employer regarding wages and working conditions. Industrial unions include workers in a particular industry, e.g., the automobile industry. Craft unions include workers with a particular skill or craft, e.g., carpenters. Legislation aims to ensure a harmonious relationship between employers and employees, with disputes being settled in an amicable manner.

Conciliation and Mediation

Sometimes, during a negotiation between management and unions, relations become strained, and it looks as though a strike or lockout is imminent. The government may employ full-time mediators to settle disputes and prevent strikes/lockouts. Alternatively, judges, lawyers, priests, university professors, or other professionals may be appointed as mediators or arbitrators.

Even when a contract does exist between management and unions, those who feel that they have been treated unfairly can file a "grievance," to be dealt with in accordance with the procedures established during collective bargaining. Contracts may be altered upon mutual consent.

When All Else Fails

When it appears that a serious dispute will not be resolved,
1. employees may go on strike or engage in picketing—i.e., discourage customers and suppliers from dealing with the firm in question or take part in a boycott wherein members of other unions and/or the public refuse to do business with the firm; or
2. owners or management may enforce a lockout—i.e., prevent workers from entering the firm's premises or obtain an injunction to prevent a strike or a picket, or form an employer's association in an attempt to deal with the matters on hand.

Some Issues in Collective Bargaining

Unions need security—certification plus support of an increasing number of members—for financial and negotiating strength within a closed shop, wherein only union members are allowed to work in a firm/industry, or a union shop, wherein employees must join the union after the probationary period. Unions focus on real wage increases—i.e., wage increases that exceed the cost of living index (COLA), reasonable hours of work, job security, promotion, and related factors.

Open Book Management (OBM): Sharing Information with Employees

Open book management is being followed in many successful business organizations and involves sharing information with employees in the hope that brainstorming and employee participation in decision making will lead to increased profitability and benefits for all.

Conclusion and Summary

Trust is important in any relationship and promotes win-win situations. Therefore, management and unions should build trust instead of engaging in acts that destroy trust, e.g., delay tactics or threats! Unions and management should engage in open communication and focus on mutual gains and simple solutions that consider the separate (and joint) interests of both parties.

Chapter 4

Women: From Here to Eternity!

The social, cultural, and political attitudes of modern society have enabled women to seize power from men! Women have an insatiable thirst to conquer fields that were once considered the sole property of men! Gender differences have contributed to women being competent leaders in the corporate world. Let us review the good and bad sides of both men and women in the workplace.

Women: The Good, the Bad, and the Ugly

Communication: Women communicate well in the business environment because of the skills they acquired as children. Women understand that fruitful conversations promote sound business relationships and teamwork, thus contributing to an improvement in the bottom line.

Organization: Women are usually well organized; they manage a dual career, as homemakers and professional employees, but may lose headway if projects do not progress according to plan.

Relationship: Women often regard their fellow employees as family and take time to ascertain their personal needs. Hence, they can sometimes be taken undue advantage of. Women tend to be detail-oriented at times, thereby causing others to get impatient for results.

Competition: Competition is strange for most women; they were not groomed for winning!

The Ugly: Some women can be overambitious at times, and this can lead to undermining the importance of corporate goals.

Men: The Good, the Bad and the Ugly

Communication: Men are direct, although Machiavelli believed in a display of power through indirectness: "Some of the things that appear to be virtues will, if [a leader] practices them, ruin him, and some of the things that appear to be vices will bring him security and prosperity."

Organization: Men grew up learning a hierarchical system; roles were assigned to everyone!

Relationship: Men do not let personal feelings hamper their progress. Their direct approach may cause unhappy employees to be spiteful.

Competition: Men are good at competing because they learned to compete as little boys. They can be vicious and may go to extremes to achieve their goals.

The Ugly: Men may try to prevent women from climbing the ladder of success!

In her book *How to Succeed in Business without a*

Penis, Karen Salmansohn stated, "How to that a woman's enemy is her super ego, whereas a man's assistant is his super ego." A woman will fear what others may say if she works overtime or is successful. Fay Weldon, a writer, stated, "Worry less about what other people think of you, and more about what you think about them." Women have been taught to conceal rather than reveal, inspire rather than aspire, emerge rather than submerge. A former mayor of Ottawa once said, "Whatever women do, they must do twice as well as men to be thought of as half as good. Luckily, this is not difficult!"

Women of the Old-School Genre

The "ideal family" consisted of a working father, a stay-at-home mother, and their children. Women who broke the rules were targets of scorn and were chastised by society:
1. Divorced women were blamed for not pleasing their men, had to enter the workforce without experience, and settle for jobs such as waitresses or cashiers.
2. Widows had to support their families while being watched by the cynics of society.
3. Women whose children worked were criticized for not providing for their families.

Due to their commitment and perseverance, these women contributed to the evolution of women.

Women of the New-School Genre

Women have advanced by destroying the barriers that society built to contain them. Today, a woman can
1. wear whatever she wants;
2. operate on patients with or without the assistance of men;

3. be recruited in the military; and
4. sit on the board of directors or even be the leader of a country!

Positive Effects of the Evolution
1. The humanitarian and charitable legacy of Mother Theresa and Princess Diana
2. Oprah Winfrey—controlling the media to voice her opinion in a very powerful manner
3. Gloria Steinem—an American feminist icon, journalist, and women's rights advocate, opened many doors for women

Negative Effects of the Evolution
1. Leona Helmsley—a real estate tycoon and hotelier who lost control of her business in the USA because of her tyrannical behavior and illegal business practices
2. Monica Lewinsky—almost destroyed the presidential career of "the most powerful" man in the world, despite his significant contribution to the USA
3. Martha Stewart—who was found guilty of insider trading

Girls were taught to be modest, polite, and nurturing. Dolls and tea sets were their main toys so they could train to become good mothers and have good relationships. On the other hand, boys were exposed to basketball, football, cops and robbers, and war games, and their aim was to win and rarely (if ever) to admit to their weaknesses! The rhyme we learned at school, said it all:

>What are little girls made of?
>Sugar and spice and all that's nice,
>What are little boys made of?
>Frogs and snails and crocodile tails.

Today, we see toy advertisements that are geared toward career-oriented females. There are toys that promote competitiveness in both genders—e.g., monopoly, scrabble, and boggle. Women engage in tennis, football, basketball, golf, boxing, and wrestling! In the office, women often wear suits, which are similar in style to those worn by men, without feeling self-conscious. Women are now voicing their opinions, standing up for equality, and gaining a strong foothold in the workplace. But the question arises: should a man give up his seat on the bus for a woman?

Margaret Thatcher once said, "One only gets to the top rung of the ladder by steadily climbing up one step at a time, and suddenly, all sorts of powers, all sorts of abilities become within our own possibility." Women took one step at a time and kept forging ahead. Perhaps it started during the Second World War when women made weapons for men to fight with and kill one another!

Politics Then

Women were not allowed to vote, and it was far-fetched to think of a woman as the leader of a nation. The political history of Germany, Russia, England, and France confirm that men can destroy humanity—"power corrupts and absolute power corrupts, absolutely." As men ruled the world, they slaughtered for the sake of country and pride. If women had a voice then, they would have talked their way out of any war!

Politics Now

Some women took gigantic leaps to become leaders of nations. Margaret Thatcher became the first female prime minister to successfully contest three general elections. Indira Gandhi was once the prime minister of India. Benazir Bhutto became the first female leader of a Moslem country. Corazon Aquino ousted Ferdinand Marcos and stabilized the chaotic state of the Philippines. Some questions, however, remain unanswered—e.g., in the USA, why are less than 20 percent of congressional representatives women even though women represent more than half the population?

Power in the Hands of Women: To Use or to Abuse?

When women start to follow in the footsteps of men by being tyrannical, anti-social, and intoxicated by power, they lose their identity and bearings. Women should focus on a diplomatic approach and learn how to exude self-confidence while maintaining self-respect and deal with the competition without being intimidated or taken undue advantage of.

Women who achieve powerful positions in the corporate world may be subjected to personal and professional attacks because of their gender. Independent women are strong, fearless, and in control of their homes, families, emotions, and their working environment. They tackle problems with a heads-on approach, being steadfast in their pursuit of success and happiness.

Professional Women: Independent and Single versus Independent and Married

Independent and Single

These women are strong-willed and focus on climbing the corporate ladder. They often deny the need for a husband and/or children and complications related thereto, without realizing that they may seek companionship during their twilight years.

Independent and Married
These women have succeeded in balancing a family life with a professional career while being (duly) supported by the love of their husband and children.

The Ladder of Success: Barefoot and Pregnant to Chairperson of the Board

Barefoot and Pregnant
These women were groomed to please their man, have children, and accept physical and mental abuse with few avenues to turn to for help.

Chairperson of the Board
In order to climb the corporate ladder, women had to work twice as hard as men, and some were taken undue advantage of. Women successfully lobbied government agencies and lawmakers to introduce laws to protect their rights against discrimination and harassment in the workplace. In order to succeed, women must have substance and style while being able to network with influential people within the organization and on the outside.

Sexual Harassment in the Workplace
Sexual harassment—i.e., any unwelcome sexual advance or inference—is unethical; it defies positive corporate culture! Women entering the workforce encountered this problem while trying to adjust to an environment that was ruled by men. After years of concealing their experiences (because of embarrassment), they began pushing for laws to prevent such behavior.

Women in the Information Era

If the Industrial Revolution was a man's era, the information revolution is a woman's era, as stated by Naisbitt and Aburdene in their book *Megatrends 2000*. Women are finally breaking through the "glass ceiling," becoming leaders and starting businesses of their own.

During the Industrial Revolution, high school education was enough to perform tasks in accordance with management's instructions with minimal feedback. Today, information technology demands an educated workforce. It is no longer feasible for information to be centralized in the hands of management!

The Educated Woman

Many women are graduates from reputable educational institutions. According to the book *Megatrends 2000*, about 25 percent of professionals on Wall Street are women and about 50 percent of accountants are women.

Historically

Initially, man was the provider; woman was the homemaker—today, women play both roles! With the emphasis on knowledge and information, jobs are accessible to both sexes. Firms are trying to be more sensitive to the needs of working parents by providing them with better child-care facilities, child-care allowances, and flexible parental leave options.

Since the 1930s and 1940s, several exceptional women have made their presence felt in politics, medicine, writing, and other fields: Eleanor Roosevelt, Hillary Clinton, Margaret Thatcher, Indira Gandhi, Benazir Bhutto, Corazon Aquino, Helen Taussig, and Lillian Hellman, to name a few.

Other Matters for Consideration

Both men and women have legitimate complaints! Married men feel trapped between work and family, divorced men are labeled as lousy fathers, and single men are confused by the protocol of dating. Working men are haunted by the thought of being accused of sexual harassment; unemployed men feel a sense of loss of identity and self-esteem. Men demonstrate their capacity to love by protecting and providing!

It is sexist to assume that most women are "naturally submissive to, brainwashed by, or afraid of men!" Women who are more likely to take maternity leave are less likely to move up the corporate ladder.

Conclusion

Men and women should operate as a team, both within a corporate environment and outside one with synergy in mind. Members of either gender should not feel threatened by the presence or performance of the opposite sex. It is important for men and women to realize their differences, as outlined in this chapter, and to "dance their way through corporate life," while always keeping an eye on the bottom line. What we need is a positive approach to life and business in an attempt to increase personal, corporate, national, and international welfare.

Chapter 5

Business Continuity Planning: A Team Approach

Introduction and Objective

The purpose of business continuity planning (BCP) is to ensure that the business continues successfully despite any interruptions—e.g., fire, flood, bad weather, a virus, a burglary, power failure, a terrorist attack, etc. Management should focus on continued success of the business, instead of "merely reacting to a business interruption." A company must review (on a continuous basis) the continuity/recovery of manufacturing, packaging, warehousing, shipping, customer support, and other operations that are critical to the company's survival.

A business continuity plan (BCP) is a set of instructions of what to do or not to do on an ongoing basis. It is created to ensure
1. that the company remains effective and
2. that a crisis does not become a disaster. BCP and disaster recovery should be integrated into improved

methods, business processes, and operations on a continuous basis to boost performance.

Organizations rarely invest adequately in BCP, which is considered to be an insurance policy for unlikely events rather than a positive contributor to the bottom line! Moreover, BCP is thought provoking, time-consuming, and needs buy-in from management and those involved in the preparation, implementation, and usage of the BCP.

Approach

Consider the potential impacts of each type of disaster. Every aspect of the plan must be managed to ensure that the BCP does not fall short when most needed. There are tools to help—e.g., the BCP generator, an intelligent disaster recovery plan template and guide to BCP.

Management Commitment: An Absolute Must!

The firm must incorporate BCP within the strategic business plan, thereby affirming its value.

Critical Business Functions

Assuming management support, you must identify the company's sources of revenue—e.g., ABC receives orders for widgets, builds and installs them, provides service and support, bills customers, and pays employees so that the process may continue. Secondary functions include ordering parts, paying for them, and the overall running of ABC.

Having defined the critical business functions, you must perform a risk assessment analysis for each of them and for the infrastructure supporting them. Analyze dependencies—e.g., a non-critical business function could be supporting a critical one, and consider the magnitude of the risks, their likelihood, and impact. Security controls should be commensurate with risks and justified on the basis of cost-benefit analysis.

The responsible managers should access this info and rank each business function based on criticality (considering quantitative and qualitative factors) subject to CEO approval. Users understand the tasks involved in the business functions, and the facilitator oversees the process. BCP writers must ensure continuity after recovery of the function.

Risk Assessment and Business Impact Analysis

What are you trying to protect, against whom, what, how, and at what cost? Risk assessment involves identifying threats, vulnerabilities, risks (including natural disasters and acts of employees, whether based on malice or negligence), and the business impact of a disruption—e.g., loss of revenue, customers defecting to the competition, damaged reputation, or disgruntled employees, if the company cannot pay them. A risk assessment can show whether there is vulnerability to the risk, e.g., a snowstorm in Bombay/Mumbai or a drought in London.

Annualized Loss Expectancy (ALE) = Single Loss Expectancy (SLE) × Annualized Rate of Occurrence (ARO). The ALE for a threat (with an SLE of $1 million), which is expected to occur only about once in ten thousand years, is $1 million divided by ten thousand or only $100. When the expected threat frequency (ARO) is factored into the equation, the risk is more accurately portrayed and forms the basis for meaningful cost-benefit analysis.

Annualized Rate of Occurrence (ARO) is the frequency with which a threat is expected to occur—a threat occurring once in ten years has an ARO of 0.10 a threat occurring fifty times in a given year has an ARO of 50.0.

Exposure Factor (EF) measures the magnitude of loss/impact on the value of an asset, as a percentage.

Information

An organization needs certain information in order to conduct its business—e.g., accounts payable, inventory control, payroll, etc. Information is an intangible asset; its loss could result in loss of confidentiality, market share, or even a compromise of national security. At this time, ABC is interested in the following:

1. monetary exposure—the cost to ABC if the function could not be performed
2. customer exposure—the loss of market share if the function were suspended
3. legal and regulatory exposure—Is ABC required to perform the function?
4. intra-company dependencies—How does suspension of the function affect other critical activities?

Rank the entities whose loss could adversely affect ABC's business, gain consensus from each business process core team (as discussed under the Delphi Method later in this chapter), and present the results to upper management for agreement. Some threats have a time component—e.g., a power failure that lasts a few minutes may not be a disaster, but one that lasts a few hours could well be!

Recovery Time and Recovery Point Objectives

As part of risk assessment, the Delphi teams, i.e., business process core teams, estimate the downtime of an entity, how old the information supplied by the entity can be, and how much of it can reasonably be lost when it is made available again. That is, they determine the recovery time objective (RTO) and the recovery point objective (RPO).

Recovery Time Objective

This refers to the recovery window or time interval between the occurrence of an event and the process becoming active again.

Recovery Point Objective
This refers to the freshness window or point in time at which the data must be recovered; obsolete info is useless. The teams consult management to confirm their decisions.

RTO and RPO: Related but Different

If a plastics manufacturing plant cannot make any products for a day, this may not be a problem, unless liquid plastic cools in the pipes and machinery while systems are down—recovery costs could be enormous! This indicates a long RTO but a short RPO. An uninterrupted power supply unit might be required to keep the plastic warm, even if the machinery is not running.

A system running a stock exchange must have an RTO of (almost) zero and an RPO of zero. Transactions can be in millions and must be serialized because they build upon one another—e.g., a client might sell/buy one stock so that he/she can buy/sell another stock or might buy a stock and sell it within minutes. One missing transaction could make every subsequent transaction wrong—i.e., if A buys a security from B, the accounts of both parties should be adjusted.

Whereas the RTO for an automated teller machine (ATM) application must be close to zero, the RPO is not as critical because the database will not wildly diverge if one or more transactions is/are missing, and the ATM can be used for reconciliation later on. Transactions made at ATMs are usually under US$1,000. Accurate records are important.

Consider other situations—e.g., if an electronic funds transfer (EFT) system is down, there are manual backup procedures, such as using a telephone or fax machine.

However, the RPO is zero because the loss of even a single multibillion yen transaction can ruin your day or career.

The longer the acceptable RTO, the lower the cost of recovery. If the RTO is ten minutes and you spend eight minutes deciding whether or not to deploy the plan, then the process must be restored within two minutes—that is, quickly!

Continuity and Recovery

RTO and RPO exist along a range—determine where each critical function should be placed.

Traditionally, you copy your computing environment from disk to magnetic tapes and store them safely. The shorter the RPO, the shorter the backup interval. If backups are running continuously, a tape system may not be suitable.

If RTO is long, order a new computer, load the tapes, and start your application. If RTO is short, have a computer on standby at a hot site or computer rental company. Consider the following:
1. Where your tape backup hardware and your tapes are and how quickly tapes go off-site?
2. Are duplicate tape copies sent via different routes?
3. Do you perform tape retrieval and restore tests?
4. Do you perform backups logically and ship them in "waves" (just in time) or all at once?
5. Is your application in an acquiesced state when you make backups?

Tape backups provide a safe copy of info in case of a disaster, e.g., someone accidentally purging or changing a file or total site destruction. The tapes and the backup hardware should be located away from the computer so that an incident affecting the computer doesn't affect the former. Different technologies can be used to meet differing downtime and data loss requirements.

Disaster Tolerance: Closing the Freshness Window

If tape backups are running continuously, then real-time technologies, e.g., online data duplication or vaulting, may be the solution. Data duplication is expensive but may be necessary—e.g., Web transactions, wire transfers, and supply chain applications. Duplication or vaulting duplicates data onto an off-site location as it is manipulated on the primary system. Vaulted data is batched and/or stored off-line and must be moved to the backup computer system's storage; replicated data is sent in near real time, possibly directly to the backup hardware, and is ready to run.

If the company is geographically dispersed and application uptime is imperative, you can have application domains at more than one site and distribute the load. Transactions can be split between multiple servers running at multiple sites.

When the load is being shared in this manner, there are no primary and secondary systems or sites, and you have the beginnings of indestructible, scalable computing. New servers can be added at any time; applications and database files can be migrated between the servers and sites as needed so that any server or any site can be taken off-line for testing, maintenance, or upgrades. Failure is undetectable except (perhaps) for application slowdown.

The Delphi Method

This involves building business process core teams consisting of information technology (IT), operations management, end-user management, applications support staff for each critical business function, and the records management department. This team-building technique is called the Delphi method, and it helps develop a clear view of the infrastructure (e.g., processes, records, IT applications) needed to help perform their business functions.

Controls

Once risks are assessed and recovery windows are determined, the Delphi teams can begin outlining possible BCPs for their functions, starting with the most critical. For each alternative plan, the Delphi teams need to calculate the ALE, plus the cost of the plan and controls.

The plan execution time is important. If the entity can be unavailable for only a few hours, but the execution time is two days, re-evaluate either the acceptable RTO or the plan itself.

Computer resources can be at a premium in a disaster; therefore, consider manual processes as an option. Also, address alternative sites, temporary personnel, hotel and meal costs, off-site records, forms storage, installation of new phone lines, and loss of reputation/goodwill in terms of costs versus benefits.

When a crisis occurs, a response team composed of executives and an emergency response team(s) consisting of Delphi team members determine if a disaster should be declared, the estimated downtime, the recovery window, and the time it will take to execute the plan. If the recovery window is two days and the entity will be unavailable for one day, a disaster should not be declared unless the entity is down longer than initially expected, considering the time required to execute the BCP. (The appointed spokesperson should talk to the media when necessary. After recovering from an incident, firms must communicate with customers, suppliers, employees, stakeholders, or affected public; otherwise, there will be a loss of trust and business.)

Documentation and Standards

Before developing a BCP, you need documentation for each process: change control procedures, standard operating procedures, run books, dataflow diagrams, problem isolation procedures, and a tape backup or rotation schedule, i.e., a detailed understanding of daily activities.

You must also gather specific information about your company's business functions—e.g., find out if sufficient application downtime is scheduled to back up the databases or if the software enables online backup. Is there an archival process to remove inactive records from hard copy files and databases so that they are kept at a manageable size? Also, identify where critical records are being stored: on-site, off-site, or out of the region.

The Delphi teams must be aware of any non-IT-related infrastructure required to keep each of their functions running—e.g., special paper, printers, or inks. Some questions to be answered relate to the storage and accessibility of important phone numbers, hard drives, and removable media.

The BCP planner must develop/purchase a standard set of forms and procedures to be used by each function, thereby enabling coordination.

The Disaster Recovery Institute (DRI) International promotes BCP and provides a certification program, incorporating standards for best practice. DRI has replaced the designation "Certified Disaster Recovery Planner" (CDRP) with "Certified Business Continuity Planner" (CBCP). (The Disaster Recovery Journal is dedicated to the field of disaster recovery and business continuity and sponsors two annual conferences in the USA.) DRI defines seven phases of a BCP program: project initiation, functional requirements, design and development, implementation, testing and exercise, maintenance and update, and execution.

1. Project initiation phase (objectives and assumptions). The main objective is to ensure that a firm can satisfy stakeholders and other parties at all times and at a reasonable cost.
2. Functional requirements phase (fact gathering, alternatives, and management decisions). Before developing a BCP, which identifies activities to be performed during a disaster scenario, you must understand each process and have documentation for change control procedures, standard operating procedures, run books, dataflow diagrams, problem isolation procedures, and a tape backup or rotation schedule.
3. Design and development phase (designing the plan). All business leaders must be involved in designing the BCP because the board of directors is held responsible in times of crises. The BCP must consider each business process and recognize interdependencies across them.
4. Implementation phase (creating the plan). The corporate team, consisting of a primary and secondary contact from each department, performs the centralized tasks common to all business functions, thus eliminating duplication of effort while the plans are being written and easing resource contention during an actual disaster.

   The corporate team maintains a list of resources required for each business function's plan (based on forms filled in and submitted by the latter) and resolves conflicts. If you have chosen a PC-based disaster recovery package, the software must suit your BCP or be adapted accordingly. In the event of a disaster, the security department may start the actual notification process.

A responsibility list is a checklist, by job function/team, of what each person will be required to do during the seven phases of plan execution - evaluation, notification, emergency response, interim processing, salvage, relocation/re-entry, and resumption of normal processing.
5. Testing and exercise phase (post-implementation plan review). Test the plan through realistic "war game" exercises: roadblocks, new events, and conditions to ensure that recovery procedures are adequate. These sessions should precede hands-on testing of the plan and provide an unbiased evaluation of how well the BCP would protect essential locations, processes, people, and technology. Once designed and tested, it is important to revaluate the plan, improve it, and re-test it because business processes change in line with corporate requirements.

In a crisis situation, there must be a good crises communication plan, and management should be accessible. The communication and PR people must deal with the press, the media, the stakeholders, and other parties.
6. Maintenance and update phase. Consultants/others should audit the BCP frequently, e.g., through workshops, to ensure that it is current and incorporates best practice. Certain tool kits contain checklists, questionnaires, etc., to examine BCP and support arrangements and perform a "dependency analysis," assessing resource dependencies and time criticalities.
7. Execution phase (when disaster occurs). Document expectations from key employees: work during outages, potential travel, work beyond normal business hours, and reporting, etc.

8. You must have a guide that contains the following:
   a. Step-by-step approach for each group to follow in writing the BCP
   b. Corporate team description and availability of resources to assist each business function in developing its BCP
   c. Notification process, plan considerations, and a responsibility list

The continuity planner maintains the first-level response part of the plan, including lists of important phone numbers, at the corporate level.

There are issues that must be addressed by business functions as they write their plans. You must assign the tasks necessary for recovery to teams or by job titles rather than to named individuals (because of employee turnover) while the plan is being written rather than in the midst of a disaster! A responsibility list is a checklist, by job function/team, of what each person will be required to do during the seven phases of plan execution:

1. Evaluation. Based on the situation and the criteria for declaring a disaster, determine whether a disaster should be declared and what parts of the plan to deploy.
2. Notification. The notification process should be followed as detailed in the plan.
3. Emergency response. Activate your hot site, relocate people and equipment, pull supplies from storage, hire temporary personnel, notify the media, stop trading in your stock, etc.
4. Interim processing. Continue running your business as effectively as possible.
5. Salvage. The damage assessment team must salvage the maximum from the primary site after pictures are taken and insurance issues are handled. Equipment, microfilm, paper, and magnetic media

degrade rapidly if not properly removed, stored, and recovered. If restoring the site is not feasible, should the company relocate?
6. Relocation/re-entry. Move out of the emergency site to its previous/new facility. Enter any manually generated information into your automated systems.
7. Resumption of normal processing. At the end of plan execution, your company's business functions return to normal. Remember to debrief everyone involved in plan execution and update and test the plan as necessary.

Writing the BCP

Develop the BCP written by employees within each business function; employees know the day-to-day activities and different functions can be generating plans at the same time, thereby providing buy-in of the plans. Staff should be available to answer questions as each group writes its BCP. Each business function and department represented on the corporate team needs to have a plan in case they are affected by the disaster. The plan can be written online but must also be stored on paper to help ensure accessibility.

Responsibilities of the Corporate Continuity Planner (CCP)

The CCP must supply each business function and each corporate team member with a BCP binder with plan dividers and a phone list: office, home, mobile, and pager numbers for each corporate team member, backup person, and manager, plus the phone numbers for police, fire, ambulance, hospital, hazardous materials team, government authorities, and utilities. These binders store each business function's BCP upon approval by the CCP and the auditors.

Executives are given an emergency phone list, an executive phone list, and a plan execution "quick start" document.

Corporate team members must keep a copy of the binder, with their own BCP and requirements sheets from each business function appended, at home and in their offices. The various business functions select a primary and a backup contact to care for their own plans, which should also be stored at home, locally, and at the backup site. The CCP has copies of each corporate team member's and business function's BCPs and must ensure that these copies can be retrieved at all times, with copies being maintained safely on-site and off-site in data storage vaults.

Working with Local Authorities

During the development of the BCP, invite local police, fire, hazardous materials, and utilities (such as power and water) personnel so that they become familiar with your facility prior to a disaster situation. Thus, you can find out if elements of your plan conflict with those of other companies or with rules in effect during a regional disaster declaration. When it is time to exercise the BCP, consider inviting the authorities (again) to participate.

Building (Business Process) Teams

This was discussed earlier in this chapter as part of the Delphi method.

Building a Corporate Team and Demonstrating Team Effort

Build a corporate team consisting of support staff from various departments of the firm. After a disaster, these employees must continue their support roles and implement changes to the affected areas, e.g., legal, public relations and others. Owners, managers, and users must cooperate in the preparation and implementation of the BCP.

BCP should be exercised frequently, with problems being solved and feedback being encouraged, to ensure that the BCP works and reflects best practice. BCP exercises should demonstrate viability, capture relevant issues, and educate participants on their roles/responsibilities during a "disaster" while building a bond between individuals with different roles in the organization and helping them contribute to corporate development.

Prior to the BCP exercise, management should
1. select scenario(s) to be tested through simulation, and identify all participants in the exercise;
2. schedule the BCP exercise(s) and all participants in an appropriate facility; and
3. communicate roles, responsibilities, and expectations to all participants involved.

Participants

1. An independent BCP management consultant/other individual who is responsible for
   a. keeping the session flowing in a timely manner with discussions, questions, and feedback;
   b. introducing relevant "roadblocks" during the exercise; and
   c. ensuring issues are documented and discussing next step activities and time frames.
2. Recovery team members with assigned tasks and responsibilities within the BCP:
   a. The business BCP must be reviewed prior to the exercise.

b. The responsible parties must discuss proposed actions based on the disruption scenario and related time frames.
   c. The owner(s)/manager(s) must be involved in the BCP exercise and must monitor progress.
3. A scribe to document the proceedings of the BCP exercise, including discussions and amendments.
4. Observers—Management, internal/external audit teams, other departments/sites, regulatory agencies, business partners, or key clients may participate in the BCP exercise at an appropriate facility, e.g., the conference room.

Scenarios

The BCP consultant and management should discuss several disruption scenarios—e.g., power failure, fire, computer breakdown, hacking, malicious damage to physical/intellectual property, malicious acts of employees, slowdown in government services like a delay in issuing permits/licenses, theft, flood, etc.—and the agenda for the exercise should include the following:
1. Overview of objectives and approach
2. Introduction of participants and roles
3. Business process(es) overview
4. Presentation of scenario
5. Description of team procedures and assigned tasks
6. Evaluation of BCP and strategies
7. Review of issues, amendments/corrective actions, and responsible parties
8. Repetition of 4 to 7 for next scenario (if appropriate), plus closing discussion and next steps

Rules

1. The facilitator will table any issue for resolution through a positive approach, based on team effort, with silence being considered an agreement on issues.

2. The scenario will change as and when necessary, with no outside interference being permitted.

Facilitator Leading Questions
The BCP consultant must ensure that the BCP exercise is fruitful through questions, discussions, and "roadblocks" created to test the recovery teams and eliminate weaknesses in the BCP plan.

Introduction
Are all participants present, have they reviewed the BCP information relevant to their areas of operation, and do they understand their role(s) in the BCP exercise?

Scenario Presentation
Does everyone understand the disruption scenario? Document questions or assumptions that we should agree upon (as a group) before proceeding.

Simulation Exercise
1. Who decides to activate the BCP, on what basis, and who prompts the initiation of BCP tasks?
2. Who does what, in what sequence, how long before the next step can be taken, and can we speed up recovery?
3. Are there any anticipated bottlenecks, and do we have an alternative plan?
4. Who else needs to be notified, are they mentioned in the plan, and is contact info current? Have all resources been assigned to recovery? What if a key resource/person is unavailable?
5. Is the plan sufficiently detailed: steps, processes, resources, and strategies? If not, who will rectify this situation?
6. Are we now "back in business?" If so, then how do we proceed?

7. When does this contingency procedure become a problem, and how must we deal with it?
8. How do we ensure accuracy and completeness of all records and return to normal?

Closing
Have we dealt with all issues and concerns? Who is responsible for updating each BCP?

Evaluation
Results of the exercise should be presented, discussed, and acted upon to ensure recovery and continued success!

Common Findings
1. BCP documentation requires update and/or more detail.
2. Sequence of BCP tasks and strategies needs review.
3. A backup person for all key BCP tasks is (often) required.
4. Awareness, emphasis, and training programs need customization and improvement.
5. The tabletop BCP exercise is cost-effective and increases awareness with minimal disruption. The BCP should not contain critical gaps or ignore contingencies/risks, e.g., security breaches or malicious actions. One reason for gaps in planning and preparedness is the failure of CEOs to realize that BCP affects every aspect of operations—e.g., stakeholders and the community—rather than merely the IT department. Therefore, managers and users (of the BCP) must liaise with all departments when preparing and implementing a BCP.
6. Insurance and financial services companies and regulators of critical industries, i.e., those closely tied

to the welfare of consumers, may insist on adequate protection against disruptions in order to qualify for coverage of losses.
7. The preparation of a strong risk management program can be broken down as follows:
   a. Identify which processes, products, locations, lines of business, and departments should be highlighted in the BCP. Prepare a list of resource needs in the face of a disruption—e.g., personnel, computer hardware/software, communications technology, office space, equipment, and supplies—and note ideal recovery times for incidents.
   b. Test the plan through realistic "war game" exercises, which include roadblocks, new events, and conditions to ensure that existing recovery procedures are comprehensive. These sessions should precede hands-on testing of the plan and provide an unbiased evaluation of how well the BCP would protect essential locations, processes, people, and technology. Once designed and tested, it is important to re-evaluate the plan, improve it, and retest it because business processes change in line with corporate requirements.
   c. Implement an incident management infrastructure: coordinate reporting (to stakeholders, the media, and other outsiders), response, transportation, external communications, e-mail, facilities, legal actions, loss control, and resources during and after a disaster. List the assignments and responsible parties: CEO, legal counsel, and staff during an incident.
   d. Train employees in crisis management through classroom sessions based on the firm's operations.

Business continuity specialists, i.e., those who help prepare and implement the BCP, must be current in their knowledge of best crisis management practices by being active in the contingency planning exchange and similar groups.

Compliance with ISO 17799, a major international standard on business continuity and disaster recovery planning, is becoming mandatory. ISO 17799 has ten major sections: BCP, systems access control, system development and maintenance, physical and environmental security, compliance, personnel security, security organization, computer and operations management, asset classification and control, and security policy.

e. Set benchmarks for business disruption preparedness/recovery to ensure that BCP is effective against disasters, including a virus, a fire, a flood, bad weather, an earthquake, a terrorist attack, etc. Event assessment, reporting, and action plans must be prepared within two to forty-eight hours of an incident. Employees must have a basic understanding of crisis management policies and procedures based on a sufficient number of practical classroom sessions and disaster drills. Suppliers, customers, and other parties related to the company must also have effective BCPs.

Information must be relevant, accurate, timely, and secure; otherwise, the firm may face penalties.

8. BCP and disaster recovery should be integrated into improved methods, business processes, and operations on a continuous basis to boost performance. Certain issues need to be resolved.

a. Delegate responsibility for BCP to a manager/consultant who has a thorough understanding of business processes and needs. Consider the potential impact of each type of disaster and set up a BCP to minimize the impact within a cost-benefit approach.
b. Determine the current status of the existing BCP. Identify the gap between requirements and the BCP and determine whether the associated risks are acceptable.

The benefits of a new system can be reaped only if the users are sold on it, as confirmed by the experience at Cedars-Sinai Medical Center, USA, where doctors and staff rebelled against a (computerized) patient-care system because they were unprepared for the changes in work flow.

Other Matters

An Amateur (ham) Radio Organization

If your company belongs to an amateur radio club/association, the lattter will help with recovery efforts. While you use your security radios in business recovery, amateur radio volunteers can be called on to assist with human safety issues.

Application Availability Requirements

If risk analysis shows that your computer application cannot be down even for routine maintenance, your systems must allow for online upgrade and maintenance.

Backup and Restore Process

1. Back up files in the order in which they need to be restored.
2. Pull and ship files from your off-site storage in "waves" so that the most critical files arrive sooner. While the next set of tapes is being pulled, the first set can be on its way to the recovery site. Duplicate

tapes must be shipped separately so that transportation accidents do not delay business recovery.
3. Determine how many tape drives are required at the backup site to meet your RTO.
4. One firm cut file-restoration time by 50 percent by optimizing tape usage; tape is inexpensive.
5. Automate your recovery tasks so that mistakes are minimized.

Audit of the BCP
This should be conducted as discussed earlier, in the maintenance and update phase.

Security
Security should be addressed by business management, IT, and other staff and should relate to potential impacts, threats, and existing vulnerabilities; otherwise, there could be unnecessary expenditure. Companies must maintain certain "baseline" standards due to legislation—e.g., the data protection act, enterprise policy, regulatory controls, etc. Risk analysis methodology should enable rapid identification of any failings in this matter.

Consistency
Risk analysis brings a consistent and objective approach to all security reviews and all systems rather than merely the IT systems. Consultative, Objective, and Bifunctional Risk Analysis (COBRA) is a comprehensive questionnaire-based (professional) PC system, using "expert" system principles and an extensive knowledge base consisting of risk analysis, consultative, and security review tools to handle the changing nature of security. COBRA mandates that security reviews be cost-justified without the constraints of lack of expertise, time, and finance.

COBRA recognizes that business users should be involved in risk analysis, evaluates the relative importance of all threats and vulnerabilities, and generates appropriate solutions. Risks identified are automatically linked with their potential implications, e.g., financial/customer loss for the business with a risk score/level for each category of risk.

COBRA risk consultant generates questionnaires from "knowledge base" question modules that are specifically suited to the firm, environment, and system under evaluation and can be directed to personnel with the appropriate expertise and knowledge in an attempt to obtain more info and contribute to better solutions. COBRA risk consultant can be used without detailed security knowledge or expertise in using risk management software. Reports produced are professional in nature, suitable for interpretation by both technical and non-technical management, and can be directed to paper/a terminal/a file (for import into a word-processing package.)

Service Level Agreements (SLAs) define the service in question, the basis of its delivery, the understanding between the parties involved, and their responsibilities and are an important part of business continuity management. Continuity and recovery are central to all good service level agreements. There is a website that provides a service agreement tool kit, consisting of a service level agreement template, a guide, a presentation, and a checklist, all of which are designed to help you create a quality SLA speedily.

Conclusion and Summary

Firms must have an effective BCP to minimize the adverse effects of disruptions. The location and quality of the offsite disaster facility must be carefully reviewed. Before

September 11, 2001, some firms at the World Trade Center had a backup facility nearby. Therefore, destruction of the alternative site was an obvious danger. BCP services are available from outside firms, but the firm providing BCP services may have other customers and may not be able to handle BCP problems effectively, unless the company in question is on a high-priority list!

One way to approach a BCP program is via the Delphi method—experts in each business function identify their critical business processes and develop separate (but coordinated) BCPs for each process. The benefits are the following:
1. Non-critical business processes do not hinder critical ones; thus, limited resources can be used effectively.
2. An infrastructure that supports noncritical business processes is duly taken care of.
3. Multiple critical business processes or applications can be recovered in parallel.

Applications that run on different systems can be recovered on the same system if necessary. Developing a BCP is a long-term process that requires substantial human and monetary resources companywide rather than in the IT department alone, and support from management.

Questions and Answers

Question 1: How would you define Business Continuity (BC) and Disaster Recovery (DR)?
Answer: BC is a strategic process aimed at continuous operation of the business entity, whereas DR is a process that enables a business enterprise to recover from a disaster.

Question 2: What are the phases of BCP?
Answer: Project initiation, functional requirements, design and development, implementation, testing

and exercise, maintenance and update, and execution. (You need a guide that contains a step-by-step approach for each group to follow in writing the BCP, corporate team description, and availability of resources to assist each business function in developing its plan, notification process, plan considerations, and a responsibility list.)

Question 3: How do firms deal with events that cause the BCP/DR budget to rise continuously?
Answer: The budgets of many firms allow for the unexpected. Some firms have a chargeback procedure in place, whereby the business units are charged a service fee for DR.

Question 4: We have three locations and plan to consolidate all operations out of a single location. Current BCPs use one another's sites as alternate locations. Is there a questionnaire or checklist available to elicit a response from critical units to address business requirements in their BCPs?
Answer: You may use BIA questionnaires and BCPs for each group.

Question 5: Ideally, should BCP report to information systems, operations, or internal audit?
Answer: BCP must report to risk management—chief risk officers (CROs) are responsible for managing all types of risks—financial, operational, strategic, compliance, and technological.

Question 6: What is the best practice on the frequency of plan reviews from a DR point of view?
Answer: The frequency and depth of review is vital. There is no point in having a BCP if the home phone number of a key recovery team member is incorrect or a critical change to an application/database/owner's

requirements has not been incorporated in the BCP or recovery procedures. Changes that are necessary—e.g., personnel changes and changes to business applications or processes—must be made on an ongoing basis and should be incorporated within the BCP.

In a "best practice" world, change management should be nearly automatic; as production (people, process, or technology) changes, so do the plans—e.g., employee turnover, a manual process becomes automated, a new system is introduced, physical location moves, new phone switches/area codes, etc. Plans should be reviewed monthly with an emphasis on ongoing change management for key people, process, or technology changes midstream.

Question 7: How should firms handle employee safety after a disaster? Are there any "best practices" when it comes to assuring employees that are at the designated meeting site after a disaster?
Answer: There must be electronic ID cards to enter the building and floor wardens who keep track of employees at the office. Employees must know where (a primary and an alternate site) to meet in the event of an evacuation, and the wardens must ensure the former
that they are responsible for presenting themselves at the meeting place. Employees must be required to dial a specified telephone number (listed on an emergency card and distributed to all associates prior to a disaster) when they arrive home to be updated on the current status of the event. Associates must also have the contact information for their supervisors and vice versa. When a disaster occurs, area monitors or wardens must ensure that employees follow evacuation procedures. If someone is left inside the disaster area due to injury or disability, this matter should be duly reported by the area monitor upon reaching

the safe area. Security guards and/or emergency response team members should be trained in CPR/first aid and must assist in handling injuries. List in advance any semi-ambulatory employees, their assigned safe area, and their cell phone number.

Taking attendance is not foolproof because at the time of the evacuation, some employees may have been absent, e.g., at lunch or have gone to a doctor's appointment. Employees who are not in their designated safe area must report their presence to the area monitor so that information can be relayed to their assigned safe area. A buddy system might prove helpful. If one buddy makes it to the safe area, he/she might know the whereabouts of a missing staff member.

Question 8:   How do I determine whether or not my vendors have a BCP/DR program?
Answer: Probing is required. A request for a copy of the vendors' recovery plan may be refused on the grounds of confidentiality. Validate key items even if you get the recovery plan.

Communication—How will the vendor notify you of a disaster and its impact? What provisions has the vendor made for you to contact them in a disaster?

Provisioning—Does the vendor have a plan to reestablish the receipt, storage, and delivery of materials and service? What would be the lead time between receiving orders and delivery?

Data—Does the vendor have a plan to capture and secure critical information (contracts, accounts receivable, accounts payable, order/fulfillment information, etc.) and to make this information available on a short—or long-term basis? Does the vendor make copies/backups of this information and keep it in a secure location?

Insurance—Does the vendor or your organization have adequate insurance coverage to limit the exposure to your organization? (Your organization might have to pay a premium for materials or services if the vendor defaults during a disaster.) This is a basic approach that can be taken to interview a vendor, i.e., build your questions.

Question 9: What is the primary role and purpose of a steering committee for BCP/DR planning? What representation should reside on the steering committee to ensure effectiveness?
Answer: A BCP Steering Committee (SC) should support a BCP/DR initiative. This SC should be comprised of a team leader, a representative from each line of business, and other support group reps (e.g., audit, security, etc.) and have an executive sponsor. The SC must maintain ongoing support and viability for the BCP program, support the change management occurring as a result of the BCP implementation, and make global decisions that affect BCP enterprise-wide.

Question 10: Is there a best practice on the distance between the primary and alternate data storage site(s)?
Answer: Due to the variables in each firm and regional risks, this question is difficult to answer.

Question 11: In the event of a disaster, how do we ensure that all employees show up?
Answer: The company should do the following:
   a. Document expectations about key employees regarding work during outages, potential travel, and work beyond normal business hours.
   b. List the roles that will be required during outage: facilities manager, disaster recovery coordinator, heads of the crisis response teams, etc.

c. Be specific about roles and responsibilities during the outage—where the employees should report, within what time frame, and which resources they should bring with them, etc.
d. Create a specific policy for overtime pay,
e. If the company does have an outage, try to do something "after the event" to show your appreciation for the employee's dedication to the company.

Question 12: Has there been any trend in using personal residences as work relocation sites?
Answer: Yes, "knowledge workers" often use their residences as alternate work sites, aided by computers and access to the Internet, and this is related to flex-scheduling and managing remote employees by using e-mail messaging, Net meeting tools, and group conference lines to facilitate work group productivity. Many companies have made arrangements with schools, churches, and other similar organizations to set up alternate sites in return for a fee/compensation.

Question 13: What is a business BCP?
Answer: A business BCP is a set of instructions of what to do or not to do on an ongoing basis. It is created to ensure (a) that the company remains effective and (b) that a crisis does not become a disaster.

Question 14: How long does it take to create a business BCP? How much will it cost?
Answer: This depends on the size and complexity of the firm, but benefits should exceed costs.

Question 15: Why should I use a business BCP?
Answer: Experience shows that a good BCP ensures effectiveness and survival.

Also, note the following:
a. Banks, investors, insurers, customers, and other stakeholders will take a company that has a BCP seriously.
b. BCP assures employees that the business is trying to protect their safety and place of work.
c. BCP is about responsible management in terms of safety and financial viability.

Question 16: Does a small company need a BCP?
Answer: Yes, to combat fraud, theft, sabotage, flooding, fire, IT and utility failures, etc.

Question 17: How should a company communicate a business BCP to its employees?
Answer: In simple words, emphasizing the company's commitment to BC management.

Question 18: What systems should be in place to assist with a quick recovery program?
Answer: Keep backups and copies of documents off-site and have a plan that focuses on your critical activities and an alternative work site.

The Aberdeen Group, USA, founded in 1988, is a leading research firm serving major corporate technology end-users around the world and is the trusted advisor to the Global 5000 for value chain strategies and technology advice. The Aberdeen report confirmed that 75 percent of all firms are increasing their usage of the Internet specifically for customer sales and service. The Aberdeen Group also confirmed that average revenue lost from Internet business disruptions is now approximately $2 million per incident.

Case Studies

A recent survey by META Group found that 80 percent of businesspeople believe e-mail to be more valuable than the phone for communication and records. But e-mail presents challenges—e.g., spam, circulation of salacious content, viruses, system failures, and mail bombs.

Disaster Recovery Case Study: CC West

CC West is a large press in the United States, serving Fortune 500 clients including Dell, Wal-Mart, Southwest Airlines, and 3M Company. Most orders and production traffic are sent via e-mail.

CC West knows that effective advertising and package design or presentation need a good printer. E-mail is the most critical communication mode for companies whose clients have stringent deadlines requiring quality service, a quick response, guaranteed delivery, and competitive rates. E-mail enables clients to deliver projects digitally to the printer as compared to using messenger/overnight services. If the e-mail system goes down, business virtually stops!

Interrupted e-mail costs the company their clients' trust and money. After experiencing multiple outages, e-mail continuity became a critical issue for CC West. The company needed e-mail continuity at a reasonable cost. MessageOne's Emergency Messaging System (EMS) proved to be the solution. EMS was easy to install and worked exactly as advertised.

E-mail Continuity Case Study: Bam!

Bam is an established company that relies on e-mail to correspond with their clients—including Logitech, Motorola, Micron, and Honeywell—and partners, and to send proofs of advertisements to their customers for approval and finished work to Bam's partners and vendor firms for printing, audio, or video production.

E-mail is the way we deliver our work product—from print and television ads to marketing and sales collateral and computer code. For Bam, e-mail represents revenue—it's that simple. In 2001, Bam faced an e-mail outage that proved costly. While moving corporate headquarters, Bam's Internet service provider was late with providing updated telecom connectivity facilities—leaving Bam without e-mail for four days! MessageOne's EMS proved to be the solution—low cost and like purchasing e-mail insurance—enabling e-mail connectivity and continuity to the world.

Chapter 6

Business Ethics: An Oxymoron?

Moral problems arise when organizations are faced with issues related to bribery, conspiracy, theft, marketing policies, corporate acquisitions, investments, payments to suppliers, hiring, firing, retraining employees, falsified reports, concealment of debts, insider trading, perks to executives and outsiders, and so on. Moral problems also arise when a firm tries to cut costs, e.g., building a dam (which will block a river that canoeists and vacationers have been using for years) to generate power and reduce energy costs, or providing employees with cheap and almost tasteless coffee or non-filtered water. Are the foregoing actions ethical?

Human beings must be fair in their dealings with others! It is difficult to ensure a "win-win" situation for all because there are situations that involve conflicting interests—i.e., owners, management, other employees, suppliers, customers, government organizations, and so on.

Moral problems represent a conflict between a firm's financial and social performance—i.e., its obligations to insiders and outsiders, such as protecting loyal employees, maintaining competitive markets, producing safe products, and preserving the environment.

The success of a business is often measured by its profit and cash-flow position. Employee effectiveness is often measured by contribution to the bottom line. A salesperson who bribes purchasing agents may succeed in increasing sales and commissions. Likewise, the design engineer who finds questionable ways to cut material costs may receive more praise than one who focuses on product quality and consumer safety.

Moral Standards

Every individual has his/her moral standards—based on upbringing, values, norms, beliefs, religion, cultural background, and goals—that help him/her to judge what is "fair" and whether anyone's rights are being compromised. But moral standards are somewhat subjective!

1. *Personal goals*—If A's goal is more money and power and B's goal is more justice and equality, then A and B will differ in their opinion of what is right and what is wrong.
2. *Personal norms*—Norms relate to expectations of behavior and may lead to judgments of what is right and wrong.
3. *Personal beliefs*—Beliefs are related to norms—e.g., smoking is bad for your health; therefore, do not smoke in my presence because I value my health and so should you.
4. *Personal values*—Values reflect priorities between our goals, norms, and beliefs.

Recognizing Moral Impact

Moral problems arise when decisions result in gains for some individuals and financial/emotional/other losses for others. Therefore, when analyzing a problem, determine who will benefit/suffer and whose rights will be recognized/denied. Review the feedback of everyone involved based on their moral standards, and present the problem as a question rather than as a statement so that it does not threaten the welfare of any of the individuals concerned.

Ethical Duties

Every member of society has obligations toward others—no lying, cheating, stealing, and so on; otherwise, the (moral) foundation of a society will be destroyed even if the overall gain to society exceeds the overall loss! Review the examples outlined below:

1. *Cruise ships and the disposal of waste.* Cruises offer enjoyment, but there are problems resulting from the waste created by crew and customers. Human waste is stored in large tanks and pumped into waste treatment plants when the ships return to their home ports. *Nonhuman waste, including garbage and laundry plus the washing of utensils, is stored in smaller tanks and dumped into the sea at night.* Officials of cruise lines claim that they cannot afford larger tanks for nonhuman waste and its treatment because this would reduce space available for crew and passengers and increase costs, prices, and the number of cruises offered to the public. This would reduce the amount spent by customers on the islands they visit, thereby reducing the income of those countries. The World Health Organization (WHO) has not done much to reduce pollution resulting from this practice while maintaining that there is no proof of deterioration in health!

2. *Napster and the free exchange of recorded music.*

Downloading of music from the Internet may reduce sales revenues to distributors and recording artists. Some people maintain that downloading music, like sharing books, makes music more accessible and may result in increased sales through added exposure. Perhaps downloading should be subject to a fee of which a percentage should be forwarded to the recording artists and authorized distributors.

3. *Satellite dishes and stealing television signals.* Is it fair to buy illegal satellite dishes on the grounds that major suppliers of cable television "charge too much"?

Moral Analysis and Economic Outcomes

Moral standards differ between individuals depending upon their upbringing, traditions, religion, social and economic situations, and so on. Therefore, state the "moral" problem in a simple manner and review feedback so that an acceptable decision can be made with minimal overall harm/loss—i.e., we are concerned with "Pareto optimality," which is related to the net balance of benefits over harm for society as a whole.

The Moral Basis of Economic Theory

Economic theory is concerned with the efficient utilization of resources to satisfy consumer wants and to maximize profit and satisfaction. Pareto optimality exists at the point where it is impossible to make any given individual better off without harming another given individual. Although most businessmen believe that profits and cash flow are very important, there has been a move toward the recognition of social responsibility.

The Moral Objections to Economic Theory

The blind pursuit of profit has resulted in bribes, environmental problems, injured workers, unsafe products, closed plants, and so on—this is unethical.

Firms attempt to operate at the point where marginal revenue equals marginal cost. Each firm is located between a "factor" market for inputs (material, labor, capital, and time) and a product market, e.g., for its output of goods and services. Individuals have preference functions, aimed at maximizing their satisfaction from a limited mix of products. The forces of supply and demand create an equilibrium position for the market for all goods and services.

The Moral Claims of Economic Theory: Effectiveness

1. Firms use resources in a way that help them maximize their revenues from the usage of limited resources (materials, labor, capital, and time).
2. The forces of supply and demand determine the distribution and the market prices of the goods and services being offered by firms.
3. The political processes of society help determine the income of each consumer.
4. If managers and owners of resources act to maximize profits and consumers act to maximize satisfaction, "Pareto optimality" will exist—i.e., the greatest output and supply of goods and services with the least input of resources and the best possible prices!

Pragmatic Objections to Economic Theory

Many highly respected professionals mention the following issues:

1. *Exclusion of segments of society.* Minorities and the poor have great difficulty in maximizing their satisfaction, but this is due to economic and political factors.
2. *Presence of injurious practices.* These practices include discrimination on the basis of race, gender,

or other factors, bribery, pollution, the existence of workplace hazards, and other practices that are outside the confines of normal economic theory.
3. *Unsafe products.* This is especially common in the automobile industry—e.g., gas tanks poorly located, faulty tires, poorly designed automatic transmissions, and so on.
4. *The absence of perfect competition.* This is largely because of the business practices of larger and more powerful business organizations.

The World Bank is a transnational organization founded in 1946 and headquartered in Washington, DC, to fund development projects throughout the world and speed up global modernization. The World Bank is funded by its member nations and has the ability to borrow large sums from the capital markets in New York, London, Frankfurt, Singapore, and Tokyo at reduced rates because borrowings are guaranteed by member nations. These funds are loaned at higher rates of interest for (worthy) development projects.

The board of directors is dominated by Western countries. In 1991, Lawrence Summers, the chief economist at the World Bank, suggested that pollution, which exists in richer countries, should be transferred to poorer countries where there was not much demand for clean air and amenities! This caused an uproar because it ignored the extent to which the poorer countries should be compensated for the inward transfer (if acceptable) and to what extent!

Similarly, a proposal to pave a wilderness and build a parking lot will result in a conflict between those who prefer the preservation of the wilderness and those who prefer more parking facilities. The resulting struggle will be hard fought, with possible political moves and manipulation by both parties involved in the conflict.

Moral Analysis and Legal Requirements

How do we find a balance between financial and social performance? How do we decide what is "fair" or "just" or "right"? The law in a democracy lays down *minimum* moral standards (as a result of the goals, norms, beliefs, and values of individuals, small groups, and larger organizations) in an attempt to regulate the behavior of individuals and organizations. The rules are published, accepted, followed, and enforced by the governing bodies—e.g., the courts and the police force—with a view to ensuring the smooth running of society. Everyone should abide by the law and contribute to a *positive* change in the latter.

Incentives spur employees to focus on financial goals, for obvious reasons, unless social goals—e.g., providing employment to "less privileged" individuals—are part of the bottom line.

Reward System

A formal system may exist to reward employees who demonstrate ethical behavior.

Ethics Committee

An ethics committee may be set up to develop, update, and enforce the code of ethics.

Judiciary Board

This independent group is responsible for discovering and solving ethical problems.

Employee Training in Ethics

Training in "ethics" may include seminars, workshops, and other methods.

Johnson Controls and gender equality. Some heavy metals, e.g., lead, may adversely affect a woman's body before or during pregnancy. Therefore, companies with industrial processes that require the use of such metals may ignore (employment) applications from women of childbearing age in order to avoid legal problems.

Johnson Controls Inc., a manufacturer of lead-acid batteries for automobiles, required evidence of surgical sterilization before employing women less than or equal to fifty-five years of age. The court overruled their requirement on the grounds of discrimination and held that
1. women should be made aware of the dangers to which they subject themselves; and
2. employers would not be liable to women as long as the latter were duly informed of the risk and as long as negligence (on the part of the employer) could not be proved.

Moral Analysis and Ethical Duties

Morality refers to standards of behavior by which people are judged. Moral standards differ between
1. individuals based on upbringing, culture, education, and other factors;
2. groups, e.g., the approach to environmental protection will differ between public interest groups and business managers;
3. individuals and groups of different time periods; and
4. countries, e.g., the attitude of the USA versus the attitude of some third world countries toward environmental protection.

Members of a group do have a moral responsibility toward the well-being of one another. If people act selfishly, life will be "solitary, poor, nasty, brutish, and short," according to Thomas Hobbes, an eminent philosopher. Ethics refers to our beliefs, but it is linked to morality—e.g., smoking is bad for one's health; therefore, people should not smoke in a crowded room!

Centuries ago, three Greek philosophers laid the foundations in the matters of politics, ethics, and the "good life."
1. Socrates believed that success is equal to happiness plus contentment plus prosperity;
2. Plato emphasized that having a "good society" is equal to having a good life, which is equal to contentment plus prosperity plus justice with minimum interference and the pursuit of excellence; and
3. Aristotle focused on ethics and the need to have "good people"; therefore, happiness based on reason plus the pursuit of excellence is not equal to pleasure, wealth, or fame.

The Principle of Utilitarian Benefits
The principle of utilitarian benefits involves creating the greatest net benefits for society. We are concerned with financial and other benefits including friendship, knowledge, health, love, and so on. This principle focuses on results and treats each individual equally, i.e., the greatest good for the greatest number.

The Principle of Universal Duties
The Principle of universal duties is concerned with looking at people as ends rather than as means to an end—i.e., people should be treated with dignity, respect, and moral worth in an honest manner.

The Principle of Distributive Justice
This principle is based on truth, justice, and cooperation between all members of society to promote economic and social benefits for all—individual effort/merit is downplayed and one is not required to help anyone.

The Principle of Contributive Liberty

This principle states that no individual should interfere with the rights of any other individual/group. Therefore, non-voluntary exchanges or gifts would be unacceptable. This principle does not address the need for people to contribute to the welfare of others.

Trust, Commitment, and Other Factors

Cooperation between owners, employees, and those associated with the firm—e.g., customers, suppliers, banks, government authorities, and others—is necessary for corporate success.

Managers should be moral in order to build *trust*, thus leading to increased profits and cash flow through team effort and cooperation. If employees do not trust managers, they may not share their ideas with the latter because

1. they will not care for the welfare of the company or
2. they fear they will not receive credit for their ideas or
3. their ideas may lead to improvements in processes and layoffs, or
4. all of the above!

Managers should encourage employees to be moral instead of exerting undue pressure on them to deceive others—e.g., other employees, customers, suppliers, potential investors, society, the government, and the world. Automobile manufacturers must meet mileage, safety, and emission standards and provide training and health care benefits for their employees.

Johnson and Johnson (J&J) manufactures health care products and pharmaceutical drugs, including Band-Aid, Tylenol, surgical instruments, and sophisticated diagnostic systems.

J&J's mission statement focuses on corporate duties rather than financial gains. Several years ago, someone mysteriously put tablets containing arsenic in unsold Tylenol bottles on store shelves in Chicago and the suburbs. Six people died, but there was no proof as to whether the manufacturing plant in New Jersey or the retailers had been negligent. *Within a few days, J&J removed their packages of Tylenol from every store in the world at a cost of approximately US$100 million and replaced them free of charge, in tamper proof containers, to all retailers and customers who returned unused portions of packages of Tylenol! J&J explained that this was an indication of their responsibility toward doctors, nurses, patients, and all other customers.*

A Business Organization Should Be Moral

Overemphasis on the bottom line can lead to short-term gains at the expense of medium— and long-term profits. Managers must consider their moral obligations to employees, customers, suppliers, the government, society, and the world in general. Top management and others should have integrity and character; otherwise, the firm will fold just like a tree that rots from the top! Philosophers usually divide ethical theories into the following areas:

1. *Human rights and the prevention of cancer*. Every individual has the right to be protected from developing cancer by the acts/omissions of another person and to be informed of cancer-related matters that may affect him/her.

   Erin Brockovich, a lawyer's assistant, discovered some *medical records* while looking through a *real estate* file. She investigated the matter and uncovered massive pollution caused by a gas compressor station located in Hinkley, California, and operated by Pacific

Gas and Electric Company. The story concerns litigation due to contamination (cancer-causing hexavalent chromium), how it got into the people's water supply, subsequent actions, and the result.

In Di Palma vs. Air Canada, it was held that an employee should have adequate working conditions, including enough fresh air in circulation without secondhand smoke!

2. *Employee equity—no discrimination.* The law attempts to ensure fair treatment for all in terms of protection and benefits—i.e., no discrimination on the basis of race, origin, nationality, gender, age, physical characteristics, marital status, religion, or any disability. In certain cases, performance must be enhanced by appropriate aids to employees. Sometimes it may appear that the company is being discriminatory—e.g., evaluating foreign credentials or asking employees over the age of forty to attend certain medical examinations. The employer should be able to justify this requirement; otherwise, a lawsuit may follow! At other times, a company may appear to be nondiscriminatory by distributing literature and displaying signage to this effect.

3. *A livable environment.* We must contribute to a healthy environment including safe production processes, waste control and disposal, emissions, etc.

4. *Advertising and promotion.* Advertising and promotion should be conducted in an honest manner. Advertisements should reflect the truth, and this includes health warnings related to cigarettes and food products—e.g., fat, trans fat, sodium, and cholesterol content.

5. *Negotiations.* Is lying acceptable if the motive and results are fair?

6. *Business approaches.* General Electric (GE) aims to reduce greenhouse emissions and improve energy efficiency by 30 percent by the end of 2008 and 2012, respectively. By infusing $1.5 billion into research and development (R&D), GE proved that this project is more than a publicity blitz.

Consistency: Aligning Corporate Social Responsibility with the Business Plan

Consistency ensures that the bottom line is not compromised. Wal-Mart is known for poor wages and inadequate health care coverage, which are consistent with its low (price and) margin business model. To compensate employees, they are offered stock options based on performance.

In the USA, Wal-Mart also pushed for a higher federal minimum wage. Wal-Mart moved toward social responsibility by cutting energy use and pressuring distributors and suppliers into being more fuel-efficient. The decision to be ecologically friendly is more in synch with its business model. Starbucks, whose employees receive full health care benefits, was praised for its efforts to lobby for improved medical compensation packages.

Ethical Challenges in Human Resources (HR)

Ethics is about asking questions even if they are potentially disturbing! In the Enron/Arthur Andersen scandals, no one dared ask the questions that might have saved these companies. Now, corporations are conscious of the risks associated with failing to question the numbers!

The negative exposure that companies like Nike and Levi Strauss & Co. have experienced concerning working conditions in their Asian plants reflects unethical business practice.

HR must ensure adequate risk assessment—selection and recruitment processes, training policies, programs, appraisal systems, compensation, incentives, benefit determination, talent management systems (including manpower and succession planning), labor relations, etc. There must be programs in place to monitor age, sex, and gender discrimination, employee attitudes and morale, and talent procurement and retention. Pay attention to health, safety, termination, downsizing policies, demographics about who gets promoted, raises, and bonuses. Do potential employees see the company as a great place to work in? Are we in control of liabilities? Is there a formal (validated) system in place that is clearly understood and communicated? Has the system had unintended effects? Has it been analyzed for adverse effects, e.g., a possible discriminatory impact on legally protected groups? Is there a formal assessment of the key capabilities/talents needed in the company? Are retention rates being monitored for criticality? Do they include competitive practices, capabilities, and performance? To what degree is the expertise of key people captured by the organization? Are there noncompetitive agreements with key technical people? Does our reward system lock key contributors into the firm?

Look at the succession planning system and see how it relates to business strategy. Ask what metrics are used, and how they relate to needed capabilities. How do we monitor for derailment? Is there a fair and effective system of mentoring and coaching? As regards training policy, who participates? What are the purposes of the programs, and how are they tied in with business strategy and ethical and legal issues and evaluated? Are there gender, race, or age biases regarding attendance?

Did we use validated instruments for identifying and selecting the "right" people? To what extent is an effort made at portraying our company as a great place to work? Are the retention packages for key personnel and others tied to performance appraisal? How do we monitor satisfaction? Several companies double their sales while halving their workforce. Taking undue advantage of people is unethical!

One cannot underestimate the value of spontaneous conversations among employees. Such conversations are unlikely to occur with outsourced and contingent workers!

An Aristotelian Take on Business Ethics

Aristotle was a practical, business-oriented philosopher who asked ethical questions. Aristotle maintained that motivation is a powerful indicator of the degree to which virtue is present in our actions. Miami hoteliers cannot claim credit for sunny days, and leaders in Silicon Valley get no (ethical) credit for providing jobs that are accidentally developmental.

A leader should create an environment that allows members of an organization to realize their full potential. Jefferson paraphrased this in the Declaration of Independence when he noted that a new country should provide conditions in which all citizens could pursue happiness.

Aristotelian Questions for Corporate Leaders

1. Am I behaving in a virtuous manner? How would I want to be treated?
2. To what extent can employees learn and develop their talents and potential?
3. To what extent do all employees participate in the decisions that affect their own work and in the financial benefits resulting from their own ideas and efforts?

Aristotle believed that leaders should observe decent limits on their own power in order to allow others to develop. Leadership should be shared and rotated, with leaders satisfying owners and employees. Many successful corporate leaders consciously reject such measures of performance as inappropriate, impractical, and irrelevant to the task of creating wealth. They believe that their responsibility is to their shareholders rather than to their employees.

The Distribution of Rewards in Organizations

Aristotle discussed the role of leaders in terms of the work environment they provide for employees and the principle of rewarding people in proportion to their contributions.

Top executives often protect their compensation packages while cutting training budgets, the number of employees, benefits, and reneging on contributions to pension funds. It is considered uncivil to raise issues of distributive justice in the interests of investors and executives. Managers should place themselves in the shoes of other employees. Is the CEO the only qualified person willing and able to do the job for an astronomical salary plus options?

Examples of Aristotelian Business Leadership

By focusing on the link between contributions and rewards, directors can create a more virtuous/productive sense of community among owners, managers, and other employees.
1. In 2000, a businessman named Charlie Butcher shared the proceeds of the sale of his company with his employees in proportion to the length of their employment, giving a $55,000 check on average to each worker. (In contrast, when Daimler Benz acquired Chrysler, Chrysler shareholders and executives got

fat checks, but hourly workers got nothing.) Butcher always offered employees high starting salaries, flexible workweeks, and the opportunity to switch jobs to find a fulfilling one. Finally, Butcher sold the company to S. C. Johnson & Son Inc., despite higher offers from other companies, because the latter promised to continue the employee-friendly culture and job security he had created.

2. In 1996, David Sun and John Tu sold their company to a Japanese bank for $1.5 billion. Sun and Tu would continue to run the business and reinvest a half billion to fund future growth. They divided 10 percent of the sale among their 523 employees, with whom they had been sharing 10 percent of the profits all along. They practiced participative management, whereby all employees could contribute their full talents to the company. Why did they do this? "The issue is really not money . . . it's how you respect ...and treat ... people. It's all about trust," Tu told the *New York Times*. In 1998, just when the Japanese bank was due to make its last $333 million payment to Sun and Tu, they asked the bank to forgo the payment because the company had underperformed during the previous year. The deal was then restructured, and the postponed final payment was linked to performance. Tu explained that profits follow in the long-term when a company behaves ethically toward its partners, vendors, customers, and employees.

Sexual Harassment

Sexual harassment is unethical because it prevents people from focusing on corporate goals. Sexual harassment law was originally drafted in order to protect women from sexual pressure and unwanted attention from men, i.e., a "hostile work environment." When men continually make lewd comments, tell off-color jokes, and so on, they make women feel uncomfortable.

Men have sometimes felt sexually harassed by other men even though everyone involved was heterosexual. At a car dealership in Colorado, for example, the sales managers typically referred to salesmen as "little girls" and "whores."

Conclusion

There are many managers who are guilty of paying mere "lip service" to the concept of ethics. This is unacceptable and must not be tolerated, regardless of the circumstances.

Bibliography

The Best Business Books Ever: The 100 Most Influential Business Books You'll Never Have Time to Read. New York: Perseus Publishing, 1993.

Adams, Bob. *Streetwise Business Tips: 200 Ways to Get Ahead in Business, Most of Which I Learned the Hard Way.* Holbrook, MA: Adams Media Corporation. 1998.

Adelsberg, David and Trolley, Edward A. *Running Training like a Business.* USA: Berrett-Koehler. 1999.

Asman, David and Adam Meyerson. *The Wall Street Journal on Management.* New York: Dow Jones-Irwin. 1985.

Bacharach, Bill. *Values Based Selling.* USA: Aim High Publishing. 1996.

Blanchard, Ken & Bowles, Sheldon. *Raving Fans.* USA: William Morrow & Co. 1993.

Blanchard, Ken & Oncken Jr., William. *The One Minute Manager Meets the Monkey.* USA: Quill. 1989.

Belding, Shaun. *Dealing with the Customer from Hell.* USA: Stoddart Publishing Co. 2000.

Brinkerhoff, John R. *101 Common Sense Rules for the Office.* USA: Stackpole Books. 1992.

Caroselli, Marlene. *The Language of Leadership.* USA: Human Resource Development Press. 1990.

Chater, Kerry. *The Equality Myth.* USA: Allen & Unwin. 1995.

Drucker, Peter. *Managing for the Future: the 1990s and Beyond.* USA: Dutton. 1992.

Drucker, Peter & Maciariello, J. *The Daily Drucker.* USA: Harper Collins. 2004.

Drucker, Peter. *What We Can Learn from Japanese Management.* USA: Harvard Business Review. 1985.

Glaser, Connie B. *More Power to You.* USA: Warner Books. 1995.

Griffin, Trenholme & Daggatt, Russell. *The Global Negotiator.* USA: Harper Business. 1990.

Handy, Charles. *The Gods of Management.* USA: Oxford Press. 1995.

Handy, Charles. *Inside Organizations.* USA: Penguin. 1999.

Heim, Pat. *Smashing the Glass Ceiling.* USA: Simon & Schuster. 1995.

Holloran, James. *Why Entrepreneurs Fail.* USA: Liberty Hall Press. 1991.

Iacone, Salvatore. *Write to the Point.* USA: Career Press. 2003.

Jackson, Donna. *How to Make the World a Better Place for Women in 5 Minutes a Day.* USA: Hyperion, New York. 1992.

LaRue Tone Hosmer. *The Ethics of Management.* USA: McGraw Hill. 2006.

Lin-Grensing, Pophal. *Human Resources Management for Small Business.* USA: International Self-Counsel Press. 2000.

MacKenzie, Alec. *The Time Trap.* USA: Amacom. 1990.

Mackoff, Barbara. What Mona Lisa Knew. USA: Contemporary Books. 1990.

Miller, Michael. *Management Secrets of The Good, The Bad & The Ugly.* Canada: Winding Stair Press. 2002.

Mindell, Phyllis. *A Woman's Guide to the Language of Success.* USA: Prentice Hall. 1995.

O'Brien, Virginia. *The Fast Forward MBA in Business.* USA: John Wiley & Sons. 1996.

Peters, Thomas. *In Search of Excellence.* USA: Harper & Row. 1988.

Pinto, Maxwell. *The Management Syndrome: How to Deal with It!* UK: Minerva Press and USA: Xlibris. 2009.

Pinto, Maxwell. *Management: Flirting with Disaster!* USA: RoseDog Books. 2005.

Pophal, Lin-Grensing. *Human Resources Management for Small Business.* USA & Canada: Self-Counsel Press. 2002.

Smith, Andy & Sinclair, Annette. *What makes an Excellent Virtual Manager?* England: Roffey Park. 2003.

Strunk W & White, E. B. *The Elements of Style.* USA: Longman. 2000.

White, Kate. *Why Good Girls Don't Get Ahead but Gutsy Girls Do.* USA: Warner Books. 1995.

Verzuh, Eric. *The Fast Forward MBA in Project Management.* USA: John Wiley & Sons. 1999.

Weiss, David S. *In Search of the Eighteenth Camel.* Canada: IRC Press. 2003.

Walton, Mary. *The Deming Management Method.* USA: The Berkeley Publishing Group. 1986.

Wilder, Lilyan. *Professionally Speaking.* USA: Simon & Schuster. 1986.

Yasutaka, Sai. *The Eight Core Values of the Japanese Businessman.* USA: International Business Press. 1996.

Sources Of Articles

Infocon Magazine Issue One, October 2003 IWS Copyright © 2000-2003. Article by John Hayes: *Business Continuity Planning Tabletop Exercise White Paper*, Winter 2000.

Article by Mark D'Angelo and William Spooner on *Business Continuity Planning.*

The Best Business Books Ever, Perseus Publishing, USA 2003

Designing Controls into Computerized Systems. FitzGerald, Jerry and Ardra 1990, Jerry FitzGerald and Associates.

Disaster Recovery Planning. Toigo, Jon William. 1999, Prentice-Hall, ISBN 0-13-084506-X.

Data Replication: Tools & Techniques for Managing Distributed Info, Buretta, Marie 1997, John Wiley & Sons.

Mark Quigley: Business Continuity: *Q & A for the Enterprise,* The Yankee Group 2002

Disaster Recovery Journal, Editorial Advisory Board: *Questions & Answers by Individual Members of the EAB.* Copyright © 2004 Forsythe Technology, Inc

2003 Ernst & Young LLP, 2003 Hewlett-Packard Development Company, L.P., Iron Mountain Headquarters

MessageOne—a Leader in Business Continuity and Disaster Recovery Solutions-James O'Toole at the Markkula Center for AppliedEthics, Business and Organizational Ethics.

About the Author

DR. MAXWELL S. Pinto is an established management consultant, with a PhD in business administration from Pacific Southern University, California, USA. He is also a member of the Institute of Chartered Accountants (England and Wales) and a life member of the Institute of Professional Managers and Administrators (UK). Dr. Pinto is listed in Marquis Who's Who in the World and in several publications of the International Biographical Centre, Cambridge, England.

Dr. Pinto is fluent in several languages, with experience in management consulting, corporate analysis, management information systems, training and development, valuation and sale of business, raising venture capital, administration, and finance. Dr. Pinto believes that sound theory promotes desirable practice and that there is always room for improvement.

Dr. Pinto conducts lectures and seminars in business management, human resource management, business ethics, business law, marketing research, economics, and accounting for undergraduates, graduates, experienced businessmen, and professionals.

This book is a follow-up to his highly acclaimed and authoritative manuals on business management, *The Management Syndrome: How to Deal with It!* and *Management: Flirting with Disaster!*

Management: Tidbits for the New Millennium! is the result of Dr. Pinto's disillusionment with the approach adopted by managers all over the world. As an independent consultant, Dr. Pinto has a specific commitment toward working with businessmen, managers, and other professionals in a bottom-line approach to solving their problems.